Study Guide

for

Research Methods and Statistics
A Critical Thinking Approach

Sherri L. Jackson
Jacksonville University

THOMSON

WADSWORTH

Australia • Canada • Mexico • Singapore • Spain • United Kingdom • United States

Printed in the Canada.
1 2 3 4 5 6 7   06 05 04 03 02

Printed by Webcom.
0-534-55424-5

For more information about our products, contact us at:
Thomson Learning Academic Resource Center
1-800-423-0563

For permission to use material from this text, contact us by:
Phone: 1-800-730-2214
Fax: 1-800-731-2215
Web: www.thomsonrights.com

Asia
Thomson Learning
5 Shenton Way #01-01
UIC Building
Singapore 068808

Australia
Nelson Thomson Learning
102 Dodds Street
South Street
South Melbourne, Victoria 3205
Australia

Canada
Nelson Thomson Learning
1120 Birchmount Road
Toronto, Ontario M1K 5G4
Canada

Europe/Middle East/South Africa
Thomson Learning
High Holborn House
50-51 Bedford Row
London WC1R 4LR
United Kingdom

Latin America
Thomson Learning
Seneca, 53
Colonia Polanco
11560 Mexico D.F.
Mexico

Spain
Paraninfo Thomson Learning
Calle/Magallanes, 25
28015 Madrid, Spain

Contents

Preface

This study guide provides you with some tools to help you master the material in the text book. Each chapter of the study guide is organized into several sections. First is a **chapter outline** followed by a **chapter summary**. **Learning objectives** are then presented followed by a **glossary of important terms** from the chapter with their definitions. You should review the glossary of terms so that you could, if asked, explain them to someone else. Next, **summary matrices** from the text book are presented. You should review the material in the summary matrices before taking the self-tests later in the chapter. For chapters with inferential statistics (Chapters 6 & 8-10), a **review of formulas** that were learned in the text book chapter follows the summary matrices. The self-tests appear next. There are several types of self tests. In every chapter there is a **fill-in self test** and a **multiple choice self test**. They vary in length depending on the length of the chapter. For those chapters with inferential statistics, **self test problems** follow the multiple choice self test. There is typically one problem for each type of statistic discussed in the chapter. Answers to all of the self tests are presented next. Lastly, at the end of each chapter there is a list of **key terms**. Use the list as a final means of quizzing yourself on the concepts presented in the chapter.

I hope that you find some of this information helpful in preparing for your class. Should you desire to contact me concerning anything in this study guide, my email address is sjackso@ju.edu.

Sherri L. Jackson

Chapter 1
Thinking Like a Scientist

Chapter Outline

Chapter Summary

The chapter begins by stressing the importance of research in psychology. This includes identifying different areas within the discipline of psychology in which research is conducted, such as human development, cognition, psychobiology, social psychology, and psychotherapy. In addition, various sources of knowledge are discussed including intuition, superstition, authority, tenacity, rationalism, empiricism and the scientific method. The importance of using the scientific method to gain knowledge in psychology is also stressed. The scientific method is a combination of empiricism and rationalism; it must meet the criteria of systematic empiricism, public verification, and posing solvable problems.

The three goals of science (description, prediction, and explanation) are discussed and related to the research methods used by psychologists. Descriptive methods include observation, case study, and survey methods. Predictive methods include correlational and quasi-experimental methods. The experimental method allows for explanation of cause-and-effect relationships. Finally, the chapter introduced some practicalities of doing research, discussed proof and disproof in science, and noted that testing a hypothesis involves attempting to falsify it.

Learning Objectives

- Identify and describe the areas of psychological research.
- Identify and differentiate between the various sources of knowledge.
- Describe the three criteria of the scientific (critical thinking approach).
- Explain the goals of science.
- Explain the difference between basic and applied research.
- Identify and compare descriptive methods.
- Identify and compare predictive (relational) methods.
- Describe the explanatory method. Your description should include independent variable, dependent variable, control group, and experimental group.

- Explain how we "do" science and how proof and disproof relate to doing science.

Glossary of Important Terms

Study the list of terms below so that you could, if asked, explain them to someone else.

Applied Research—The study of psychological issues that have practical significance and potential solutions.

Basic Research—The study of psychological issues in order to seek knowledge for its own sake.

Case Study Method—An in-depth study of one or more individuals.

Control Group—The group of participants that does not receive any level of the independent variable and serves as the baseline in a study.

Correlational Method—A method in which the degree of relationship between two variables is assessed.

Dependent Variable—The variable in a study that is measured by the researcher.

Description—Carefully observing behavior in order to describe it.

Experimental Group—The group of participants that receives some level of the independent variable.

Experimental Method—A research method that allows a researcher to establish a cause-and-effect relationship through manipulation of a variable and control of the situation.

Explanation—Identifying the causes that determine when and why a behavior occurs.

Hypothesis—A prediction regarding the outcome of a study, often involving the relationship between two variables in a study.

Independent Variable—The variable in a study that is manipulated by the researcher.

Knowledge via Authority—Knowledge gained from those viewed as authority figures.

Knowledge via Empiricism—Knowledge gained through observation of organisms and events in the real world.

Knowledge via Intuition—Knowledge gained without being consciously aware of its source.

Knowledge via Rationalism—Knowledge gained through logical reasoning.

Knowledge via Science—Knowledge gained through a combination of empirical methods and logical reasoning.

Knowledge via Superstition—Knowledge that is based on subjective feelings, belief in chance, or belief in magic events.

Knowledge via Tenacity—Knowledge gained from repeated ideas and stubbornly clung to despite evidence to the contrary.

Laboratory Observation—Observing the behavior of humans or other animals in a more contrived and controlled situation, usually the laboratory.

Naturalistic Observation—Observing the behavior of humans or other animals in their natural habitat.

Negative Relationship—A relationship between two variables in which an increase in one variable is accompanied by a decrease in the other variable.

Observational Methods—Make observations of human or other animal behavior.

Participant (Subject) Variable—A characteristic inherent in the participants that cannot be changed.

Population—All of the people about whom a study is meant to generalize.

Positive Relationship—A relationship between two variables in which an increase in one variable is accompanied by an increase in the other variable.

Prediction—Identifying the factors that indicate when an event or events will occur.

Principle of Falsifiability—The idea that a scientific theory must be stated in such a way that it is possible to refute or disconfirm it.

Pseudoscience—Making claims that appear to be scientific but that actually violate the criteria of science.

Public Verification—Presenting research to the public so that it can be observed, replicated, criticized, and tested.

Quasi-experimental Method—A study in which the variable of interest cannot be manipulated.

Random Assignment—Assigning participants randomly to the groups in a study.

Random Sample—A means of generating a representative sample.

Sample—The group of people who participate in a study.

Skeptic—A person who questions the validity, authenticity, or truth of something purporting to be factual.

Solvable Problems—Questions that are potentially answerable by means of currently available research techniques.

Survey Method—Questioning individuals on a topic or topics and then describing their responses.

Systematic Empiricism—Making observations in a systematic manner in order to test hypotheses and refute or develop a theory.

Theory—An organized system of assumptions and principles that attempts to explain certain phenomena and how they are related.

Variable—An event or behavior that has at least two values.

Chapter Summary Matrices

Following are the summary matrices from Chapter 1. Review the material in the matrices before taking the self-tests that follow.

Sources of Knowledge

Source	Description	Advantages/Disadvantages
Superstition	• gaining knowledge through subjective feelings, belief in chance, or belief in magic events	• not empirical or logical
Intuition	• gaining knowledge without being consciously aware of where the knowledge was gained	• not empirical or logical

Authority	• gaining knowledge from those viewed as authority figures	• not empirical or logical • authority figure may not be an expert in the area
Tenacity	• gaining knowledge by clinging stubbornly to repeated ideas, despite evidence to the contrary	• not empirical or logical
Rationalism	• gaining knowledge through logical reasoning	• logical but not empirical
Empiricism	• gaining knowledge through observation of organisms and events in the real world	• empirical but not necessarily logical/systematic
Science	• gaining knowledge through empirical methods and logical reasoning	• the only acceptable way for researchers/scientists to gain knowledge

The Scientific Method

Criteria	Description	Why Necessary
Systematic Empiricism	• making observations in a systematic manner in order to test hypotheses	• aids in refuting or developing a theory
Public Verification	• presenting research to the public so that it can be observed, replicated, criticized, and tested	• aids in determining the veracity of a theory
Solvable Problems	• stating questions in such a way that they are potentially answerable by means of currently available research techniques	• aids in determining whether a theory can be tested using empirical techniques and whether it is falsifiable

An Introduction to Research Methods

Goal Met	Research Methods	Advantages-Disadvantages
Description	• Observational Method • Case Study Method • Survey Method	• allow description of behavior(s) • do not support reliable predictions • do not support cause and effect explanations
Prediction	• Correlational Method • Quasi-experimental Method	• allow description of behavior(s) • supports reliable predictions from one variable to another • do not support cause and effect explanations

Explanation	• Experimental Method	• allows description of behavior(s) • supports reliable predictions from one variable to another • supports cause and effect explanations

Fill-in Self Test

Answer the following questions. If you have trouble answering any of the questions, re-study the relevant material before going on to the multiple choice self test.

1. To gain knowledge without being consciously aware of where the knowledge was gained exemplifies gaining knowledge via _intuition_.

2. To gain knowledge from repeated ideas and to cling stubbornly to them despite evidence to the contrary exemplifies gaining knowledge via _tenacity_.

3. A _hypothesis_ is a prediction regarding the outcome of a study that often involves a prediction regarding the relationship between two variables in a study.

4. A person who questions the validity, authenticity, or truth of something purporting to be factual is a _skeptic_.

5. _Solvable pr_ are questions that are potentially answerable by means of currently available research techniques.

6. _Pseudoscience_ involves making claims that appear to be scientific but that actually violate the criteria of science.

7. The three goals of science are _____, _____, and _____.

8. _____ research involves the study of psychological issues that have practical significance and potential solutions.

9. A _____ is an in depth study of one or more individuals.

10. All of the people about whom a study is meant to generalize are the _____.

11. The _____ method is a method in which the degree of relationship between at least two variables is assessed.

12. A characteristic inherent in the participants that cannot be changed is known as a _____ variable.

13. The variable in a study that is manipulated is the _____ variable.

14. The _____ group is the group of participants that serves as the baseline in a study. They do not receive any level of the independent variable.

Multiple Choice Self Test

Select the single best answer for each of the following questions. If you have trouble answering any of the questions, re-study the relevant material.

1. A belief that is based on subjective feelings is to knowing via _____ as stubbornly clinging to knowledge gained from repeated ideas is to knowledge via _____.
   a. authority; superstition
   b. superstition; intuition
   c. tenacity; intuition
   d. superstition; tenacity

2. Tom did really well on his psychology exam last week and he believes that it is because he used his lucky pen. He has now decided that he must use this pen for every exam that he writes because he believes that it will make him lucky. This belief is based on:
   a. superstition.
   b. rationalism.
   c. authority.
   d. science.

3. A prediction regarding the outcome of a study is to _____ as an organized system of assumptions and principles that attempts to explain certain phenomena and how they are related is to _____.
   a. theory; hypothesis
   b. hypothesis; theory
   c. independent variable; dependent variable
   d. dependent variable; independent variable

4. _____ involves making claims that appear to be scientific but that actually violate the criteria of science.
   a. The principle of falsifiability
   b. Systemic Empiricism
   c. Being a skeptic
   d. Pseudoscience

5. The study of psychological issues in order to seek knowledge for its own sake is to _____ as the study of psychological issues that have practical significance and potential solutions is to _____.
   a. basic; applied
   b. applied; basic
   c. naturalistic; laboratory
   d. laboratory; naturalistic

6. Ray was interested in the mating behavior of squirrels so he went into the field to observe them. Ray is using the _____ method of research.
   a. case study method
   b. laboratory observational
   c. naturalistic observational
   d. correlational

7. Negative correlation is to _____ as positive correlation is to _____.
   a. increasing or decreasing together; moving in opposite directions
   b. moving in opposite directions; increasing or decreasing together
   c. independent variable; dependent variable
   d. dependent variable; independent variable

8. Which of the following is a participant (subject) variable?
   a. amount of time given to study a list of words
   b. fraternity membership
   c. the number of words in a memory test
   d. all of the above

9. If a researcher assigns subjects to groups based on, for example, their earned GPA, the researcher would be employing:
   a. a manipulated independent variable.
   b. random assignment.
   c. a participant variable.
   d. a manipulated dependent variable.

10. In an experimental study of the effects of time spent studying on grade, time spent studying would be the:
    a. control group.
    b. independent variable.
    c. experimental group.
    d. dependent variable.

11. Baseline is to treatment as _____ is to _____.
    a. independent variable; dependent variable
    b. dependent variable; independent variable
    c. experimental group; control group
    d. control group; experimental group

12. In a study of the effects of alcohol on driving performance, driving performance would be the:
    a. control group.
    b. independent variable.
    c. experimental group.
    d. dependent variable.

Answers to Self Test Questions

Fill-in Self Test Answers

1. intuition (P. 6)
2. tenacity (P. 7)
3. hypothesis (P. 8)
4. skeptic (P. 10)
5. Solvable problems (P. 11)
6. Pseudoscience (P. 11)
7. description, prediction, explanation (P. 13)
8. Applied (P. 14)
9. case study (P. 15)
10. population (P. 15)
11. correlational (P. 15)
12. participant (subject) (P.16)
13. independent (P. 17)
14. control (P. 17)

Multiple Choice Self Test Answers

1. d (P. 6-7)
2. a (P. 6)
3. b (P. 7)
4. d (P. 11)
5. a (P. 13-14)
6. c (P. 14)
7. b (P. 16)
8. b (P. 16)
9. c (P. 16)
10. b (P. 17)
11. d (P. 17)
12. d (P. 17)

Key Terms

Below are the terms from the glossary presented earlier. Go through the list and see if you can remember the definition of each.

Applied Research	Naturalistic Observation
Basic Research	Negative Relationship
Case Study Method	Observational Methods
Control Group	Participant (Subject) Variable
Correlational Method	Population
Dependent Variable	Positive Relationship
Description	Prediction
Experimental Group	Principle of Falsifiability
Experimental Method	Pseudoscience
Explanation	Public Verification
Hypothesis	Quasi-experimental Method
Independent Variable	Random Assignment
Knowledge via Authority	Random Sample
Knowledge via Empiricism	Sample
Knowledge via Intuition	Skeptic
Knowledge via Rationalism	Solvable Problems
Knowledge via Science	Survey Method
Knowledge via Superstition	Systematic Empiricism
Knowledge via Tenacity	Theory
Laboratory Observation	Variable

Chapter 2
Getting Started: Defining, Measuring, and Manipulating Variables

Chapter Outline

Selecting a Problem
Reviewing the Literature
    Library Research
    Journals
    Psychological Abstracts
    PsychLIT and PsychINFO
    Social Science Citation Index
    Other Resources
Defining Variables
Properties of Measurement
Scales of Measurement
    Nominal Scale
    Ordinal Scale
    Interval Scale
    Ratio Scale
Discrete and Continuous Variables
Types of Measures
    Self-report Measures
    Tests
    Behavioral Measures
    Physical Measures
Reliability
    Error in Measurement
    How to Measure Reliability: Correlation Coefficients
    Types of Reliability
        Test Retest Reliability
        Alternate-Forms Reliability
        Split-Half Reliability
        Interrater Reliability
Validity
    Content Validity
    Criterion Validity
    Construct Validity

Chapter Summary

This chapter presented many elements crucial to getting started on a research project. It began with how to select a problem and conduct a literature search. The importance of operationally defining both the independent and dependent variables in a study was discussed. This involves defining them in terms of the activities of the researcher in measuring and/or manipulating each variable. It is also important to determine the scale or level of measurement of a variable. This may be determined by looking at the properties of measurement (identity, ordinality, equal unit size, and true zero) of the variable. Once established, the level of measurement (nominal, ordinal, interval, or ratio) helps determine the appropriate statistics for use with the data. Data can also be classified as discrete (whole number units) or continuous (allowing for fractional amounts).

The chapter also described several type of measures including self-report (reporting on how you act, think, or feel) test (ability or personality), behavioral (observing and recording behavior), and physical (measurements of bodily activity) measures. Finally, various types of reliability (consistency) and validity (truthfulness) in measures were discussed. This included discussing error in measurement, using correlation coefficients to assess reliability and validity, and the relationship between reliability and validity.

Learning Objectives

- Use resources in the library to locate information.
- Explain and give examples of an operational definition.
- Explain the four properties of measurement and how they are related to the four scales of measurement.
- Identify and describe the four types of measures.

- Explain what reliability is and how it is measured.

- Identify and explain the four types of reliability discussed in the text.

- Explain what validity is and how it is measured.

- Identify and explain the four type of validity discussed in the text.

Glossary of Important Terms

Study the list of terms below so that you could, if asked, explain them to someone else.

Absolute Zero—A property of measurement in which assigning a score of zero indicates an absence of the variable being measured.

Alternate-forms Reliability—A reliability coefficient determined by assessing the degree of relationship between scores on two equivalent tests.

Behavioral Measures—Measures taken by carefully observing and recording behavior.

Construct Validity—The degree to which a measuring instrument accurately measures a theoretic construct or trait that it is designed to measure.

Content Validity—The extent to which a measuring instrument covers a representative sample of the domain of behaviors to be measured.

Continuous Variables—Variables that usually fall along a continuum and allow for fractional amounts.

Correlation Coefficient—A measure of the degree of relationship between two sets of scores. It can vary between -1.00 and $+1.00$.

Criterion Validity—The extent to which a measuring instrument accurately predicts behavior or ability in a given area.

Discrete Variables—Variables that usually consist of whole number units or categories and are made up of chunks or units that are detached and distinct from one another.

Equal Unit Size—A property of measurement in which a difference of 1 means the same amount throughout the entire scale.

Face Validity—The extent to which a measuring instrument appears valid on its surface level.

Identity—A property of measurement in which objects that are different receive different scores.

Interrater Reliability—A reliability coefficient that assesses the agreement of observations made by two or more raters or judges.

Interval Scale—A scale in which the units of measurement (intervals) between the numbers on the scale are all equal in size.

Magnitude—A property of measurement in which the ordering of numbers reflects the ordering of the variable.

Negative Correlation—An inverse relationship between two variables in which an increase in one variable is related to a decrease in the other, and vice versa.

Nominal Scale—A scale in which objects or individuals are broken into categories that have no numerical properties.

Operational Definition—A definition of a variable in terms of the operations (activities) a researcher uses to measure or manipulate it.

Ordinal Scale—A scale in which objects or individuals are categorized and the categories form a rank order along a continuum.

Physical Measures—Measures of bodily activity (such as pulse or blood pressure) that may be taken with a piece of equipment.

Positive Correlation—A relationship between two variables in which the variables move in the same direction—an increase in one is related to an increase in the other and a decrease in one is related to a decrease in the other.

Ratio Scale—A scale in which, in addition to order and equal units of measurement, there is an absolute zero that indicates an absence of the variable being measured.

Reactivity—A possible reaction by participants in which they act unnaturally because they know they are being observed.

Reliability—An indication of the consistency of a measuring instrument.

Self-report Measures—Usually questionnaires or interviews that measure how people report that they act, think, or feel.

Split-half Reliability—A reliability coefficient determined by correlating scores on one half of a measure with scores on the other half of the measure.

Test-retest Reliability—A reliability coefficient determined by assessing the degree of relationship between scores on the same test, administered on two different occasions.

Tests—A measurement instrument used to assess individual differences in various content areas.

Validity—A measure of the truthfulness of a measuring instrument. It indicates whether the instrument measures what it claims to measure.

Chapter Summary Matrices

Following are the summary matrices from Chapter 2. Review the material in the matrices before taking the self-tests that follow.

Library Research

Tool	What It Is
Psych Abstracts	A reference resource published by the American Psychological Association that contains abstracts or brief summaries of articles in psychology and related disciplines
PsychLIT	The CD-ROM version of the *Psych Abstracts*, updated quarterly
Psych INFO	The online version of the *Psych Abstracts*, updated monthly
Social Science Citation Index (SSCI)	A resource that allows you to search for subsequent articles that have cited a key article
Interlibrary Loan (ILL)	A service provided by most libraries that allows you to borrow resources from other libraries if your library does not hold them
Sociological Abstracts	A reference that contains abstracts or brief summaries of articles in sociology and related disciplines

ERIC	A clearinghouse for research on educational psychology, testing, counseling, child development, evaluation research, and related areas.
Dissertation Abstracts	Abstracts of doctoral dissertations from hundreds of universities in the United States and Canada, published monthly

Features of Scales of Measurement

Level of Measurement				
	Nominal	**Ordinal**	**Interval**	**Ratio**
Examples	• Ethnicity • Religion • Gender	• Class Rank • Letter Grade	• Temperature (Fahrenheit and Celsius) • Many Psychological Tests	• Weight • Height • Time
Properties	• Identity	• Identity • Magnitude	• Identity • Magnitude • Equal Unit Size	• Identity • Magnitude • Equal Unit Size • Absolute Zero
Mathematical Operations	• None	• Rank Order	• Add • Subtract	• Add • Subtract
Typical Statistics Used	• Mode • Chi Square	• Mode • Median • Wilcoxon Rank-Sum test	• Mode • Median • Mean • t-test • ANOVA	• Mode • Median • Mean • t-test • ANOVA

Features of Types of Measures

Types of Measure				
	Self-report	**Tests**	**Behavioral**	**Physical**
Description	Questionnaires or interviews that measure how people report that they act, think or feel	A measurement instrument used to assess individual differences	Careful observations and recordings of behavior	Measures of bodily activity

Examples of each	• Behavioral self-report • Cognitive self-report • Affective self-report	• Ability tests • Personality tests	• Counting behaviors • Classifying behaviors	• Weight • EEGs • GSRs • Blood Pressure
Considerations	• Are participants being truthful? • How accurate are the participant's memories?	• Are the participants being truthful? • How reliable and valid are the tests?	• Is there reactivity? • How objective are the observers?	• Is the individual taking the measure skilled at using the equipment? • How reliable and valid is the measuring instrument?

Features of Reliability

Types of Reliability				
	Test/Retest	Alternate-Forms	Split-Half	Interrater
What It Measures	Stability over time	Stability over time and equivalency of items	Equivalency of items	Agreement between raters
How It Is Accomplished	Administer the same test to the same people at two different times	Administer alternate but equivalent forms of the test to the same people at two different times	Correlate performance for a group of people on two equivalent halves of the same test	Have at least two people count or rate behaviors, and determine the percentage of agreement between them

Features of Validity

	Types of Validity			
	Content	Criterion / Concurrent	Criterion / Predictive	Construct
What It Measures	Whether the test covers a representative sample of the domain of behaviors to be measured	The ability of the test to estimate present performance	The ability of the test to predict future performance	The extent to which the test measures a theoretical construct or trait
How It Is Accomplished	Asking experts to assess the test to establish that the items are representative of the trait being measured	Correlate performance on the test with a concurrent behavior	Correlate performance on the test with a behavior in the future	Correlate performance on the test with performance on an established test or with people who have different levels of the trait the test claims to measure

Fill-in Self Test

Answer the following questions. If you have trouble answering any of the questions, re-study the relevant material before going on to the multiple choice self test.

1. ________________ and ________________ are electronic versions of the Psychological Abstracts.

2. The ________________ can help you to work from a given article to see what has been published on that topic since the article was published.

3. A definition of a variable in terms of the activities a researcher used to measure or manipulate it is an ________________.

4. ________________ is a property of measurement in which the ordering of numbers reflects the ordering of the variable.

5. A(n) _____ scale is a scale in which objects or individuals are broken into categories that have no numerical properties.

6. A(n) _____ scale is a scale in which the units of measurement between the numbers on the scale are all equal in size.

7. Questionnaires or interviews that measure how people report that they act, think, or feel are _____.

8. _____ occurs when participants act unnaturally because they know they are being observed.

9. When reliability is assessed by determining the degree of relationship between scores on the same test, administered on two difference occasions, _____ is being used.

10. _____ produces a reliability coefficient that assess the agreement of observations made by two or more raters or judges.

11. _____ assesses the extent to which a measuring instrument covers a representative sample of the domain of behaviors to be measured.

12. The degree to which a measuring instrument accurately measures a theoretic construct or trait that it is designed to measure is assessed by _____.

Multiple Choice Self Test

Select the single best answer for each of the following questions. If you have trouble answering any of the questions, re-study the relevant material.

1. Gender is to the _____ property of measurement as time is to the _____ property of measurement.
    a. magnitude; identity
    b. equal unit size; magnitude
    c. absolute zero; equal unit size
    d. identity; absolute zero

2. Arranging a group of individuals from heaviest to lightest represents the _____ property of measurement.
   a. identity
   b. magnitude
   c. equal unit size
   d. absolute zero

3. Letter grade on a test is to the _____ scale of measurement as height is to the _____ scale of measurement.
   a. ordinal; ratio
   b. ordinal; nominal
   c. nominal; interval
   d. interval; ratio

4. Weight is to the _____ scale of measurement as political affiliation is to the _____ scale of measurement.
   a. ratio; ordinal
   b. ratio; nominal
   c. interval; nominal
   d. ordinal; ratio

5. Measuring in whole units is to _____ as measuring in whole units and/or fractional amounts is to _____
   a. discrete variable; continuous variable
   b. continuous variable; discrete variable
   c. nominal scale; ordinal scale
   d. both a and c

6. An individual's potential to do something is to _____ as an individual's competence in an area is to _____.
   a. tests; self-report measures
   b. aptitude tests; achievement tests
   c. achievement tests; aptitude tests
   d. self-report measures; behavioral measures

7. Sue decided to have participants in her study of the relationship between amount of time spent studying and grades keep a journal of how much time they spent studying each day. The type of measurement that Sue is employing is known as a(n):
   a. behavioral self-report measure.
   b. cognitive self-report measure.
   c. affective self-report measure.
   d. aptitude test.

8. Which of the following correlation coefficients represents the variables with the weakest degree of relationship?
   a. -.99
   b. -.49
   c. +.83
   d. +.01

9. Which of the following is true?
   a. Test-retest reliability is determined by assessing the degree of relationship between scores on one half of a test with scores on the other half of the test.
   b. Split-half reliability is determined by assessing the degree of relationship between scores on the same test, administered on two different occasions.
   c. Alternate-forms reliability is determined by assessing the degree of relationship between scores on two different, equivalent tests.
   d. None of the above.

10. If observers disagree 20 times out of 80, then the inter-rater reliability is:
    a. 40%.
    b. 75%.
    c. 25%.
    d. not able to be determined.

11. Which of the following is not a type of validity?
    a. criterion validity
    b. content validity
    c. face validity
    d. alternate-forms validity

12. Which of the following is true?
    a. Construct validity is the extent to which a measuring instrument covers a representative sample of the domain of behaviors to be measured.
    b. Criterion validity is the extent to which a measuring instrument accurately predicts behavior or ability in a given area.
    c. Content validity is the degree to which a measuring instrument accurately measures a theoretic construct or trait that it is designed to measure.
    d. Face validity is a measure of the truthfulness of a measuring instrument.

Answers to Self Test Questions

Fill-in Self Test Answers

1. PsychLIT; PsychINFO (P. 29)
2. Social Science Citation Index (SSCI) (P. 29)
3. operational definition (P. 31)
4. Magnitude (P. 32)
5. nominal (P. 33)
6. interval (P. 34)
7. self-report measures (P. 36)
8. Reactivity (P. 38)
9. test-retest reliability (P. 41)
10. Interrater reliability (P. 42)
11. Content validity (P. 44)
12. construct validity (P. 45)

Multiple Choice Self Test Answers

1. d (P. 32)
2. b (P. 32)
3. a (P. 33-34)
4. b (P. 33-34)
5. a (P. 35)
6. b (P. 37)
7. a (P. 37)
8. d (P. 40)
9. c (P. 42)
10. b (P. 43)
11. d (P. 43)
12. b (P. 44)

Key Terms

Below are the terms from the glossary presented earlier. Go through the list and see if you can remember the definition of each.

Absolute Zero
Alternate-forms Reliability
Behavioral Measures
Construct Validity
Content Validity
Continuous Variables
Correlation Coefficient
Criterion Validity

Discrete Variables
Equal Unit Size
Face Validity
Identity
Inter-rater Reliability
Interval Scale
Magnitude
Negative Correlation

Nominal Scale
Operational Definition
Ordinal Scale
Physical Measures
Positive Correlation
Ratio Scale
Reactivity

Reliability
Self-report Measures
Split-half Reliability
Test-retest Reliability
Tests
Validity

Chapter 3
Descriptive Methods

Chapter Summary

In this chapter the various ways of conducting a descriptive study were discussed. The three methods presented were the observational method (naturalistic versus laboratory), the case study method, and the survey method (mail, telephone, or personal interview). Several advantages and disadvantages of each method were discussed. For observational methods, important issues included reactivity, experimenter expectancies, time, cost, control, and flexibility. The case study method is limited by describing only one or a few people and being very subjective in nature, but it is often a good means of beginning a research project. The various survey methods may have problems of biased samples, poor return rates, interviewer biases, socially desirable responses, and expense. Various methods of sampling participants for surveys were discussed, along with how best to write a survey and arrange the questions on the survey.

Keep in mind that all of the methods presented in this chapter are descriptive in nature. They allow researchers to describe what has been observed in a group of people or other animals, but they do not allow researchers to make accurate predictions or determine cause-and-effect relationships.

Learning Objectives

- Explain the difference between naturalistic and laboratory observation.
- Explain the difference between participant and nonparticipant observation.
- Explain the difference between disguised and nondisguised observation.
- Describe how to use a checklist versus a narrative record.
- Describe an action checklist versus a static checklist.
- Describe the case study method.
- Identify the three methods of surveying.
- Identify advantages and disadvantages of the three survey methods.
- Differentiate random sampling, stratified random sampling, and cluster sampling.
- Differentiate open-ended, closed-ended, and partially open-ended questions.
- Explain the difference between loaded questions, leading questions, and double-barreled questions.

Glossary of Important Terms

Study the list of terms below so that you could, if asked, explain them to someone else.

Action Checklist—A tally sheet used to note the presence or absence of behaviors.

Checklist—A tally sheet on which the researcher records attributes of the participants and whether particular behaviors were observed.

Closed-ended Questions—Questions for which participants choose from a limited number of alternatives.

Cluster Sampling—A sampling technique in which clusters of participants that represent the population are used.

Demographic Questions—Questions that ask for basic information such as age, gender, ethnicity, or income.

Disguised Observation—Studies in which the participants are unaware that the researcher is observing their behavior.

Double-barreled Question—A question that asks more than one thing.

Ecological Validity—The extent to which an experimental situation can be generalized to natural settings and behaviors.

Expectancy Effects—The effect of the experimenter's expectations on the outcome of a study.

Interviewer Bias—The tendency for the person asking the questions to bias the participants' answers.

Leading Question—A question that sways the respondent to answer in a desired manner.

Likert Rating Scale—A type of numerical rating scale developed by Likert in 1932.

Loaded Question—A question that includes nonneutral or emotionally laden terms.

Mail Survey—A written survey that is self-administered.

Narrative Records—Full narrative descriptions of a participant's behavior.

Non-participant Observation—Studies in which the researcher does not participate in the situation in which the research participants are involved.

Open-ended Questions—Questions for which participants formulate their own responses.

Partially Open-ended Questions—Closed-ended questions with an open-ended "Other" option.

Participant Observation—Studies in which the researcher actively participates in the situation in which the research participants are involved.

Personal Interview—A survey in which the questions are asked face-to-face.

Random Selection—A method of generating a random sample in which each member of the population is equally likely to be chosen as part of the sample.

Rating Scale—A numerical scale on which survey respondents indicate the direction and strength of their response.

Representative Sample—A sample that is representative of the population.

Sampling Bias—A tendency for one group to be overrepresented in a sample.

Socially Desirable Response—A response that is given because a respondent believes it is deemed appropriate by society.

Static Checklist—A tally sheet on which attributes that will not change are recorded.

Stratified Random Sampling—A sampling technique designed to ensure that subgroups or strata are fairly represented.

Telephone Survey—A survey in which the questions are read to participants over the telephone.

Undisguised Observation—Studies in which the participants are aware that the researcher is observing their behavior.

Chapter Summary Matrices

Following are the summary matrices from Chapter 3. Review the material in the matrices before taking the self-tests that follow.

Observational Studies

Types of Observational Studies		
	Naturalistic	Laboratory
Description	Observing people or other animals in their natural habitats	Observing people or other animals in a contrived setting, usually a laboratory
Options	Participant versus Nonparticipant Disguised versus Nondisguised	Participant versus Nonparticipant Disguised versus Nondisguised
Means of Data Collection	Narrative Records Checklists	Narrative Records Checklists
Concerns	Reactivity Expectancy effects Time Money Lack of Control	Reactivity Expectancy Effects Lack of Flexibility

Survey Methods

Survey Methods	<ul><li>Mail survey—a written survey that is self-administered</li><li>Telephone survey—a survey conducted by telephone in which the questions are read to the respondents</li><li>Personal interview—a face-to-face interview of the respondent</li></ul>
Sampling Techniques	<ul><li>Random sampling—a sampling technique in which each member of the population is equally likely to be chosen as part of the sample</li><li>Stratified random sampling—a sampling technique intended to guarantee that the sample represents specific subgroups or strata</li><li>Cluster sampling—a sampling technique in which clusters of participants that represent the population are identified and included in the sample</li></ul>
Available Question Types	<ul><li>Open-ended questions—questions for which respondents formulate their own responses</li><li>Closed-ended questions—questions on which respondents must choose from a limited number of alternatives</li><li>Partially open-ended questions—closed-ended questions with an open-ended "Other" option</li><li>Rating scales (Likert scale)—questions on which respondents must provide a rating on a numerical scale</li></ul>

Concerns	• Sampling bias • Interviewer bias • Socially desirable responses • Return rate • Expense

Fill-in Self Test

Answer the following questions. If you have trouble answering any of the questions, re-study the relevant material before going on to the multiple choice self test.

1. Observational studies in which the researcher does not participate in the situation in which the research participants are involved utilize _____ observation.

2. The extent to which an experimental situation can be generalized to natural settings and behaviors is known as _____.

3. Observational studies in which the participants are unaware that the researcher is observing their behavior utilize _____ observation.

4. _____ are full narrative descriptions of a participant's behavior.

5. A _____ checklist is a tally sheet on which attributes that will not change are recorded.

6. _____ involves a tendency for one group to be overrepresented in a study.

7. When participants give a response that they believe is deemed appropriate by society then they are giving a _____.

8. Using _____ involves generating a random sample in which each member of the population is equally likely to be chosen as part of the sample.

9. _____ is a sampling technique designed to ensure that subgroups are fairly represented.

10. Questions for which participants choose from a limited number of alternatives are known as _____.

11. A numerical scale on which survey respondents indicate the direction and strength of their responses is a _____.

12. A question that sways a respondent to answer in a desired manner is a _____.

Multiple Choice Self Test

Select the single best answer for each of the following questions. If you have trouble answering any of the questions, re-study the relevant material.

1. _____ observation has greater _____ validity than _____ observation.
   a. laboratory; construct; naturalistic
   b. laboratory; ecological; naturalistic
   c. naturalistic; ecological; laboratory
   d. naturalistic; content; laboratory

2. Which of the following is true?
   a. Naturalistic observation involves observing humans or other animals behave in their natural setting.
   b. Naturalistic observation decreases the ecological validity of a study.
   c. Laboratory observation increases the ecological validity of a study.
   d. All of the above.

3. _____ is (are) a greater concern when using _____ observation because the observations are made in an _____ manner.
   a. reactivity; undisguised; obtrusive
   b. expectancy effects; disguised; unobtrusive
   c. reactivity; disguised; unobtrusive
   d. expectancy effects; disguised; obtrusive

4. Naturalistic observation is to _____ as laboratory observation is to _____.
   a. more control; more flexibility
   b. more control; less control
   c. more flexibility; more control
   d. more flexibility; less control

5. Checklists are to _____ as narrative records are to _____.
    a. more subjective; less subjective
    b. less subjective; more subjective
    c. less objective; more objective
    d. both b and c

6. A tally sheet on which attributes that will not change are recorded is a _____ checklist.
    a. static
    b. action
    c. narrative
    d. non-narrative

7. Personal interview surveys have the concern of _____ but have the advantage of _____.
    a. low return rate; eliminating interviewer bias
    b. interviewer bias; high return rate
    c. sampling bias; eliminating interviewer bias
    d. both b and c

8. Of the three survey methods discussed in the text, _____ surveys tend to have the lowest response rate and the _____ expense.
    a. mail; highest
    b. personal interview; highest
    c. telephone; lowest
    d. mail; lowest

9. Poor response rate is to _____ as interviewer bias is to _____.
    a. mail surveys; personal interview surveys
    b. mail surveys; mail surveys
    c. personal interview surveys; mail surveys
    d. telephone surveys; mail surveys

10. Rich is conducting a survey of student opinion of the dining hall at his university. Rich decided to conduct his survey by using every 10th name on the registrar's alphabetical list of all students at his school. The type of sampling technique that Rich is using is:
    a. representative cluster sampling.
    b. cluster sampling.
    c. stratified random sampling.
    d. random sampling.

11. Imagine that you wanted to assess student opinion of the dining hall by surveying a subgroup of 100 students at your school. In this situation, the subgroup of students represents the _____ and all of the students at your school represent the _____.
    a. sample; random sample
    b. population; sample
    c. sample; population
    d. cluster sample; sample

12. A question including non-neutral or emotionally laden terms is a _____ question.
    a. loaded question
    b. leading question
    c. double-barreled question
    d. open-ended question

13. Open-ended question is to _____ question as a closed-ended question is to _____ question.
    a. multiple choice; short answer
    b. short answer; multiple choice
    c. short answer; essay
    d. multiple choice; essay

14. Consider the following survey question: *"Most Americans consider a computer to be a necessity. Do you agree?"* This is an example of a _____ question.
    a. leading
    b. loaded
    c. rating scale
    d. double-barreled

Answers to Self Test Questions

Fill-in Self Test Answers

1. nonparticipant (P. 50)
2. ecological validity (P. 50)
3. disguised (P. 51)
4. Narrative records (P. 53)
5. static (P. 54)
6. Sampling bias (P. 56)
7. socially desirable response (P. 58)
8. random selection (P. 59)
9. Stratified random sampling (P. 59)

10. closed-ended questions (P. 61)
11. rating scale (P. 62)
12. leading question (P. 62)

Multiple Choice Self Test Answers

1. c (P. 51-52)
2. a (P. 51)
3. a (P. 50-51)
4. c (P. 50-52)
5. b (P. 53)
6. a (P. 54)
7. b (P. 58)
8. d (P. 56-58)
9. a (P. 56-58)
10. d (P. 59)
11. c (P. 59-60)
12. a (P. 62)
13. b (P. 61-62)
14. a (P. 62)

Key Terms

Below are the terms from the glossary presented earlier. Go through the list and see if you can remember the definition of each.

Action Checklist
Checklist
Closed-ended Questions
Cluster Sampling
Demographic Questions
Disguised Observation
Double-barreled Question
Ecological Validity
Expectancy Effects
Interviewer Bias
Leading Question
Likert Rating Scale
Loaded Question
Mail Survey
Narrative Records
Nonparticipant Observation

Open-ended Questions
Partially Open-ended Questions
Participant Observation
Personal Interview
Random Selection
Rating Scale
Representative Sample
Sampling Bias
Socially Desirable Response
Static Checklist
Stratified Random Sampling
Telephone Survey
Undisguised Observation

Chapter 4
Data Organization and
Descriptive Statistics

Chapter Outline

Chapter Summary

This chapter discussed data organization and descriptive statistics. Several methods of data organization were presented including how to design a frequency distribution, a bar graph, a histogram, and a frequency polygon. The type of data appropriate for each of these methods was also discussed.

Descriptive statistics that summarize a large data set include measures of central tendency (mean, median, and mode) and measures of variation (range, average deviation, and standard deviation). These statistics provide information about the central tendency or "middleness" of a distribution of scores and about the spread or width of the distribution, respectively. A distribution may be normal, positively skewed, or negatively skewed. The shape of the distribution affects the relationship among the mean, median, and mode. Finally, the calculation of z-score transformations was discussed as a means of standardizing raw scores for comparative purposes. Although z-scores can be used with either normal or skewed distributions, the proportions under the standard normal curve can only be applied to data that approximate a normal distribution.

Based on the discussion of these descriptive methods, you can begin to organize and summarize a large data set and also compare the scores of individuals to the entire sample or population.

Learning Objectives

- Organize data in either a frequency distribution or class interval frequency distribution.
- Graph data in either a bar graph, histogram, or frequency polygon.
- Differentiate measures of central tendency.
- Know how to calculate the mean, median, and mode.
- Differentiate measures of variation.
- Know how to calculate the range, average deviation, and standard deviation.
- Explain the difference between a normal distribution and a skewed distribution.
- Explain the difference between a positively skewed distribution and a negatively skewed distribution.
- Describe what a z-score is and know how to calculate it.
- Use the area under the normal curve to determine proportions and percentile ranks.

Glossary of Important Terms

Study the list of terms below so that you could, if asked, explain them to someone else.

Average Deviation—An alternative measure of variation that, like the standard deviation, indicates the average difference between the scores in a distribution and the mean of the distribution.

Bar Graph—A graphical representation of a frequency distribution in which vertical bars are centered above each category along the x-axis and are separated from each other by a space indicating that the levels of the variable represent unrelated and distinct categories.

Class Interval Frequency Distribution—A table in which the scores are grouped into intervals and listed along with the frequency of scores in each interval.

Descriptive Statistics—Numerical measures that describe a distribution by providing information on the central tendency of the distribution, the width of the distribution, and the shape of the distribution.

Frequency Distribution—A table in which all of the scores are listed along with the frequency with which each occurs.

Frequency Polygon— A line graph of the frequencies of individual scores.

Histogram— A graphical representation of a frequency distribution in which vertical bars centered above scores on the x-axis touch each other to indicate that the scores on the variable represent related, increasing values.

Mean—A measure of central tendency; the arithmetic average of a distribution.

Measure of Central Tendency—A number intended to characterize an entire distribution.

Measure of Variation— A number that indicates how dispersed scores are around the mean of the distribution.

Median—A measure of central tendency; the middle score in a distribution after the scores have been arranged from highest to lowest or lowest to highest.

Mode—A measure of central tendency; the score in a distribution that occurs with the greatest frequency.

Negatively Skewed Distribution—A distribution in which the peak is to the right of the center point and the tail extends toward the left, or in the negative direction.

Normal Curve—A symmetrical, bell-shaped frequency polygon representing a normal distribution.

Normal Distribution—A theoretical frequency distribution having certain special characteristics.

Percentile Rank—A score that indicates the percentage of people who scored at or below a given raw score.

Positively Skewed Distribution— A distribution in which the peak is to the left of the center point and the tail extends toward the right, or in the positive direction.

Qualitative Variable—A categorical variable for which each value represents a discrete category.

Quantitative Variable—A variable for which the scores represent a change in quantity.

Range—A measure of variation; the difference between the lowest and the highest score in a distribution.

Standard Deviation—A measure of variation; the average difference between the scores in the distribution and the mean or central point of the distribution, or more precisely, the square root of the average squared deviation from the mean.

Standard Normal Distribution—A normal distribution with a mean of 0 and a standard deviation of 1.

z-score (Standard Score)—A number that indicates how many standard deviation units a raw score is from the mean of a distribution.

Chapter Summary Matrices

Following are the summary matrices from Chapter 4. Review the material in the matrices before taking the self-tests that follow.

Data Organization

	Type of Organizational Tool			
	Frequency Distribution	**Bar Graph**	**Histogram**	**Frequency Polygon**
Description	A list of all scores occurring in the distribution along with the frequency of each	A pictorial graph with bars representing the frequency of occurrence of items for qualitative variables	A pictorial graph with bars representing the frequency of occurrence of items for quantitative variables	A pictorial line graph representing the frequency of occurrence of items for quantitative variables
Use With	Nominal, ordinal, interval, or ratio data	Nominal data	Typically ordinal, interval, or ratio data—most appropriate for discrete data	Typically ordinal, interval, or ratio data—more appropriate for continuous data

Measures of Central Tendency

	Type of Central Tendency Measure		
	Mean	**Median**	**Mode**
Definition	The arithmetic average	The middle score in a distribution of scores organized from highest to lowest or lowest to highestt	The score occurring with greatest frequency
Use With	Interval and ratio data	Ordinal, interval, and ratio data	Nominal, ordinal, interval, or ratio data
Cautions	Not for use with distributions with a few extreme scores		Not a reliable measure of central tendency

Measures of Variation

	Type of Variation Measure		
	Range	**Average Deviation**	**Standard Deviation**
Definition	The difference between the lowest and highest scores in the distribution	The average distance of all of the scores from the mean of the distribution	The squareroot of the average squared deviation from the mean of a distribution
Use With	Primarily interval and ratio data	Primarily interval and ratio data	Primarily interval and ratio data

Cautions	A simple measure that does not use all scores in the distribution in its calculation	A more sophisticated measure in which all scores are used, but which may not weight extreme scores adequately	The most sophisticated and most frequently used measure of variation

Types of Distributions

	Type of Distribution		
	Normal	Positively Skewed	Negatively Skewed
Description	A symmetrical, bell-shaped, unimodal curve	A lopsided curve with a tail extending toward the positive or right side	A lopsided curve with a tail extending toward the negative or left side
z-score transformations applicable?	Yes	Yes	Yes
Percentile ranks and proportions under standard normal curve applicable?	Yes	No	No

Review of Formulas

$$\mu = \frac{\sum X}{N} \qquad \overline{X} = \frac{\sum X}{N}$$

$$A.D. = \frac{\sum |X - \mu|}{N} \qquad \sigma = \sqrt{\frac{\sum (X - \mu)^2}{N}}$$

$$S = \sqrt{\frac{\sum (X - \overline{X})^2}{N}} \qquad s = \sqrt{\frac{\sum (X - \overline{X})^2}{N-1}}$$

$$z = \frac{X - \overline{X}}{S} \, or \, \frac{X - \mu}{\sigma}$$

Fill-in Self Test

Answer the following questions. If you have trouble answering any of the questions, re-study the relevant material before going on to the multiple choice self test.

1. A _Frequency distr._ is a table in which all of the scores are listed along with the frequency with which each occurs.

2. A categorical variable for which each value represents a discrete category is a _qualitative_ variable.

3. A graphical representation of a frequency distribution in which vertical bars centered above scores on the x-axis touch each other to indicate that the scores on the variable represent related, increasing values is a _histogram_.

4. Measures of _Central Tendency_ are numbers intended to characterize an entire distribution.

5. The _Median_ is the middle score in a distribution after the scores have been arranged from highest to lowest or lowest to highest.

6. Measures of _Variation_ are numbers that indicate how dispersed scores are around the mean of the distribution.

7. An alternative measure of variation that indicates the average difference between the scores in a distribution and the mean of the distribution is the _Average Deviation_

8. When we divide the squared deviation scores by $N-1$ rather than by N, we are using the _unbiased est._ of the population standard deviation.

9. σ represents the _pop_ standard deviation and S represents the _Sample_ standard deviation.

10. A distribution in which the peak is to the left of the center point and the tail extends toward the right is a _positive_ skewed distribution.

11. A number that indicates how many standard deviation units a raw score is from the mean of a distribution is a _z score_.

12. The normal distribution with a mean of 0 and a standard deviation of 1 is the _Standard normal deviation_

Multiple Choice Self Test

Select the single best answer for each of the following questions. If you have trouble answering any of the questions, re-study the relevant material.

1. A _____ is graphical representation of a frequency distribution in which vertical bars are centered above each category along with x-axis and are separated from each other by a space indicating that the levels of the variable represent distinct, unrelated categories.
    a. histogram
    b. frequency polygon
    c. bar graph
    d. class interval histogram

2. Qualitative variable is to quantitative variable as _____ is to _____.
    a. categorical variable; numerical variable
    b. numerical variable; categorical variable
    c. bar graph; histogram
    d. both a and c

3. Seven Girl Scouts reported the following individual earnings from their sale of cookies: $17, $23, $13, $15, $12, $19, and $13. In this distribution of individual earnings, the mean is _____ the mode and _____ the median.
    a. equal to; equal to
    b. greater than; equal to
    c. equal to; less than
    d. greater than; greater than

4. When Dr. Thomas calculated her students' history test scores, she noticed that one student had an extremely high score. Which measure of central tendency should be used in this situation?
    a. mean
    b. standard deviation
    c. median
    d. either a or c

5. Imagine that 4,999 people who are penniless live in Medianville. An individual whose net worth is $500,000,000 moves to Medianville. Now the mean net worth in this town is _____ and the median net worth is _____.
    a. 0; 0
    b. $100,000; 0
    c. 0; $100,000
    d. $100,000; $100,000

6. Middle score in the distribution is to _____ as score occurring with the greatest frequency is to _____.
   a. mean; median
   b. median; mode
   c. mean; mode
   d. mode; median

7. Mean is to _____ as mode is to _____.
   a. ordinal, interval, and ratio data only; nominal data only
   b. nominal data only; ordinal data only
   c. interval and ratio data only; all types of data
   d. none of the above

8. The calculation of the standard deviation differs from the calculation of the average deviation in that the deviation scores are:
   a. squared.
   b. converted to absolute values.
   c. squared and converted to absolute values.
   d. it does not differ.

9. Imagine that distribution A contains the following scores: 11, 13, 15, 18, 20. Imagine that distribution B contains the following scores: 13, 14, 15, 16, 17. Distribution A has a _____ standard deviation and a _____ average deviation in comparison to distribution B.
   a. larger; larger
   b. smaller; smaller
   c. larger; smaller
   d. smaller; larger

10. Which of the following is not true?
    a. All scores in the distribution are used in the calculation of the range.
    b. The average deviation is a more sophisticated measure of variation than the range, however is may not weight extreme scores adequately.
    c. The standard deviation is most sophisticated measure of variation because all scores in the distribution are used and because it weights extreme scores adequately.
    d. None of the above.

11. If the shape of a frequency distribution is lopsided, with a long tail projecting longer to the left than to the right, how would the distribution be skewed?
    a. normally
    b. negatively
    c. positively
    d. average

12. If Jack scored 15 on a test with a mean of 20 and a standard deviation of 5 what is his z-score?
    a. 1.5
    b. −1.0
    c. 0.0
    d. cannot be determined

13. Faculty in the physical education department at State University consume an average of 2000 calories per day with a standard deviation of 250 calories. The distribution is normal. What proportion of faculty consume an amount between 1600 and 2400 calories?
    a. .4452
    b. .8904
    c. .50
    d. none of the above

14. If the average weight for women is normally distributed with a mean of 135 pounds and a standard deviation of 15 pounds, then approximately 68% of all women should weigh between _____ and _____ pounds.
    a. 120; 150
    b. 120; 135
    c. 105; 165
    d. Cannot say from the information given.

15. Sue's first philosophy exam score is −1 standard deviation from the mean in a normal distribution. The test has a mean of 82 and a standard deviation of 4. Sue's percentile rank would be approximately:
    a. 78%.
    b. 84%.
    c. 16%.
    d. Cannot say from the information given.

Self Test Problems

1. Calculate the mean, median, and mode for the following distribution.
   1, 1, 2, 2, 4, 5, 8, 9, 10, 11, 11, 11

2. Calculate the range, average deviation, and standard deviation for the following distribution.
   2, 2, 3, 4, 5, 6, 7, 8, 8

3. The results of a recent survey indicate that the average new home costs $100,000 with a standard deviation of $15,000. The price of homes is normally distributed.
   a. If someone bought a home for $75,000, what proportion of homes cost an equal amount or more than this?
   b. At what percentile rank is a home that sold for $112,000?
   c. For what price would a home at the 20th percentile have sold?

Answers to Self Test Questions

Fill-in Self Test Answers

1. frequency distribution (P. 70)
2. qualitative (P. 71)
3. histogram (P. 70)
4. central tendency (P. 73)
5. median (P. 75)
6. variation (P. 77)
7. average deviation (P. 78)
8. unbiased estimator (P. 82)
9. population; sample (P. 84)
10. positively (P. 84)
11. z-score (P. 86)
12. standard normal distribution (P. 88)

Multiple Choice Self Test Answers

1. c (P. 70)
2. d (P. 70)
3. d (P. 73-76)
4. c (P. 73-76)
5. b (P. 73-76)
6. b (P. 73-76)
7. c (P. 73-76)
8. a (P. 78)
9. a (P. 78)
10. a (P. 78)
11. b (P. 85)
12. b (P. 86)
13. b (P. 86)
14. a (P. 86)
15. c (P. 86)

Answers to Self Test Problems

1. $\bar{x} = 6.25$, Md = 6.5, Mo = 11
2. range = 6, A.D. = 2, σ = 2.26
3. a. $z = -1.67$, proportion = .9525
   b. $z = +.80$, percentile rank = 78.81
   c. $87,400

Key Terms

Below are the terms from the glossary presented earlier. Go through the list and see if you can remember the definition of each.

Average Deviation
Bar Graph
Class Interval Frequency
Distribution
Descriptive Statistics
Frequency Distribution
Frequency Polygon
Histogram
Mean
Measure of Central Tendency
Measure of Variation
Median
Mode

Negatively Skewed Distribution
Normal Curve
Normal Distribution
Percentile Rank
Positively Skewed Distribution
Qualitative Variable
Quantitative Variable
Range
Standard Deviation
Standard Normal Distribution
z-Score (standard score)

Chapter 5
Correlational Methods and Statistics

Chapter Outline

Chapter Summary

After reading this chapter, you should have an understanding of the correlational research method, which allows researchers to observe relationships between variables, and correlation coefficients, the statistics that assess that relationship. Correlations vary in type (positive or negative) and magnitude (weak, moderate, or strong). The pictorial representation of a correlation is a scatterplot. Scatterplots allow us to see the relationship, facilitating the interpretation of a relationship.

When interpreting correlations, there are several errors that are commonly made. These include assuming causality and directionality, the third variable problem, having a restrictive range on one or both variables, and lastly, assessing a curvilinear relationship. Knowing that two variables are correlated allows researchers to make predictions from one variable to another.

Four different correlation coefficients (Pearson's, Spearman's, Point-biserial, and Phi) and when each should be used were discussed. The coefficient of determination was also discussed with respect to more fully understanding correlation coefficients. Lastly, regression analysis, which allow us to predict from one variable to another, was described.

Learning Objectives

- Describe the difference between strong, moderate, and weak correlation coefficients.
- Draw and interpret scatterplots.
- Explain negative, positive, curvilinear and no relationship between variables.
- Explain how assuming causality and directionality, the third-variable problem, restrictive ranges, and curvilinear relationships can be problematic when interpreting correlation coefficients.
- Explain how correlations allow us to make predictions.
- Describe when it would be appropriate to use the Pearson product-moment correlation coefficient, the Spearman rank-order correlation coefficient, the point-biserial correlation coefficient, and the phi coefficient.
- Calculation of the Pearson product-moment correlation coefficient for two variables.
- Determine and explain r^2 for a correlation coefficient.
- Explain what regression analysis is.
- Determine the regression line for two variables.

Glossary of Important Terms

Study the list of terms below so that you could, if asked, explain them to someone else.

Causality—The assumption that a correlation indicates a causal relationship between the two variables.

Coefficient of Determination—A measure of the proportion of variance in one of the variables that is accounted for by the other variable; calculated by squaring the correlation coefficient.

Correlation Coefficients—A measure of the degree of relationship between two sets of scores. It can vary between −1.00 and +1.00.

Correlational Method—A type of non-experimental research method that describes the relationship between two measured variables.

Directionality—The inference made with respect to the direction of a relationship between two variables.

Magnitude—An indication of the strength of the relationship between two variables.

Negative Correlation—An inverse relationship between two variables in which an increase in one variable is related to a decrease in the other and vice versa.

Partial Correlation—A correlational technique that involves measuring three variables and then statistically removing the effect of the third variable from the correlation of the remaining two variables.

Pearson Product-moment Correlation Coefficient—A correlation coefficient for use when both variables are measured on an interval or ratio scale.

Person-who Argument—Arguing that a well-established statistical trend is invalid because we know a "person-who" went against the trend.

Phi Coefficient—The correlation coefficient for use when both measured variables are dichotomous and nominal.

Point-biserial Correlation Coefficient—The correlation coefficient for use when one of the variables is measured on a dichotomous, nominal scale and the other is measured on an interval or ratio scale.

Positive Correlation—A relationship between two variables in which the variables move together—an increase in one is related to an increase in the other and a decrease in one is related to a decrease in the other.

Regression Analyses—A procedure which allows us to predict an individual's score on one variable based on knowing one or more other variables.

Regression Line—The line that best fits the center of a scatterplot.

Restrictive Range—A variable that is truncated and does not vary enough.

Scatterplot—A figure showing the relationship between two variables, that graphically represents the relationship between the variables.

Spearman's Rank-order Correlation Coefficient—The correlation coefficient for use when one or more of the variables is measured on an ordinal (ranking) scale.

Third Variable Problem—The problem of a correlation between two variables being dependent on another (third) variable.

Chapter Summary Matrices

Following are the summary matrices from Chapter 5. Review the material in the matrices before taking the self-tests that follow.

Types of Relationships

	Relationship Type			
	Positive	**Negative**	**None**	**Curvilinear**
Description of Relationship	**Variables increase and decrease together**	**As one variable increases, the other decreases—an inverse relationship**	**Variables are unrelated and do not move together in any way**	**Variables increase together up to a point and then as one continues to increase, the other decreases**

Description of Scatterplot	Data points are clustered in a linear pattern extending from lower left to upper right	Data points are clustered in a linear pattern extending from upper left to lower right	There is no pattern to the data points—they are scattered all over the graph	Data points are clustered in a curved linear pattern forming a U-shape or an inverted U-shape
Example of Variables Related in This Manner	Smoking and cancer	Mountain elevation and temperature	Intelligence level and weight	Memory and age

Misinterpreting Correlations

Types of Misinterpretations				
	Causality and Directionality	Third Variable	Restrictive Range	Curvilinear Relationship
Description of Mis-interpretation	Assume the correlation is causal and that one variable causes changes in the other	Other variables are responsible for the observed correlation	One or more of the variables is truncated or restricted and the opportunity to observe a relationship is minimized	The curved nature of the relationship decreases the observed correlation coefficient
Examples	Assuming that smoking causes cancer or that illiteracy causes drug abuse because a correlation has been observed	Finding a strong positive relationship between birth control and number of electric appliances	If SAT scores are restricted (limited in range), the correlation between SAT and GPA appears to decrease	As arousal increases, performance increases up to a point and then as arousal continues to increase, performance decreases

Correlation Coefficients

Type of Coefficient				
	Pearson	Spearman	Point-Biserial	Phi
Type of Data	Both variables must be interval or ratio	Both variables are ordinal (ranked)	One variable is interval or ratio and one variable is nominal and dichotomous	Both variables are nominal and dichotomous
Correlation Reported as:	$\pm$ 0.0-1.0	$\pm$ 0.0-1.0	$\pm$ 0.0-1.0	$\pm$ 0.0-1.0
r^2 Applicable?	Yes	Yes	Yes	Yes

Review of Formulas

$$r = \frac{\sum XY - \frac{\left(\sum X\right)\left(\sum Y\right)}{N}}{\sqrt{\left(\sum X^2 - \frac{\left(\sum X\right)^2}{N}\right)\left(\sum Y^2 - \frac{\left(\sum Y\right)^2}{N}\right)}}$$

$$Y' = bX + a$$

$$b = \frac{N\left(\sum XY\right) - \left(\sum X\right)\left(\sum Y\right)}{N\left(\sum X^2\right) - \left(\sum X\right)^2}$$

$$a = \overline{Y} - b\left(\overline{X}\right)$$

Fill-in Self Test

Answer the following questions. If you have trouble answering any of the questions, re-study the relevant material before going on to the multiple choice self test.

1. A _____ is a figure showing the relationship between two variables, that graphically represents the relationship between the variables.

2. When an increase in one variable is related to a decrease in the other variable and vice versa, we have observed an inverse or _____ relationship.

3. When we assume that, because we have observed a correlation between two variables, one variable must be causing changes in the other variable, we have made the errors of _____ and _____.

4. A variable that is truncated and does not vary enough is said to have a _____.

5. The _____ correlation coefficient is used when both variables are measured on an interval/ratio scale.

6. The _____ correlation coefficient is used when one variable is measured on an interval/ratio scale and the other on a nominal scale.

7. To measure the proportion of variance accounted for in one of the variables, by the other variable we use the _____.

8. _____ is a procedure which allows us to predict an individual's score on one variable based on knowing their score on a second variable.

Multiple Choice Self Test

Select the single best answer for each of the following questions. If you have trouble answering any of the questions, re-study the relevant material.

1. The magnitude of a correlation coefficient is to _____ as the type of correlation is to
   _____.
   a. slope; absolute value
   b. sign; absolute value
   c. absolute value; sign
   d. none of the above

2. Strong correlation coefficient is to weak correlation coefficient as _____ is to _____.
   a. −1.00; +1.00
   b. −1.00; +.10
   c. +1.00; −1.00
   d. +.10; −1.00

3. Which of the following correlation coefficients represents the variables with the weakest
   degree of relationship?
   a. +.89
   b. -1.00
   c. +.10
   d. -.47

4. A correlation coefficient of +1.00 is to _____ as a correlation coefficient of −1.00 is to
   _____.
   a. no relationship; weak relationship
   b. weak relationship; perfect relationship
   c. perfect relationship; perfect relationship
   d. perfect relationship; no relationship

5. If the points on a scatterplot are clustered in a pattern that extends from the upper left to
   the lower right, this would suggest that the two variables depicted are:
   a. normally distributed.
   b. positively correlated.
   c. regressing toward the average.
   d. negatively correlated.

6. We would expect the correlation between height and weight to be _____ whereas we
   would expect the correlation between age in adults and hearing ability to be _____.
   a. curvilinear; negative
   b. positive; negative
   c. negative; positive
   d. positive; curvilinear

7. When we argue against a statistical trend based on one case we are using a:
    a. third-variable.
    b. regression analysis.
    c. partial correlation.
    d. person-who argument.

8. If a relationship is curvilinear we would expect the correlation coefficient to be:
    a. close to 0.00.
    b. close to +1.00.
    c. close to −1.00.
    d. an accurate representation of the strength of the relationship.

9. The _____ is the correlation coefficient that should be used when both variables are measured on an ordinal scale.
    a. Spearman rank-order correlation coefficient
    b. coefficient of determination
    c. point-biserial correlation coefficient
    d. Pearson product-moment correlation coefficient

10. Suppose that the correlation between age and hearing ability for adults is −.65. What proportion (or percent) of the variability in hearing ability is accounted for by the relationship with age?
    a. 65%
    b. 35%
    c. 42%
    d. unable to determine

11. Drew is interested is assessing the degree of relationship between belonging to a Greek organization and number of alcoholic drinks consumed per week. Drew should use the _____ correlation coefficient to assess this.
    a. partial
    b. point-biserial
    c. phi
    d. Pearson product-moment

12. Regression analysis allows us to:
    a. predict an individual's score on one variable based on knowing their score on another variable.
    b. determine the degree of relationship between two interval/ratio variables.
    c. determine the degree of relationship between two nominal variables.
    d. predict an individual's score on one variable based on knowing that the variable is interval/ratio in scale.

Answers to Self Test Questions

Fill-in Self Test Answers

1. scatterplot (P. 101)
2. negative (P. 103)
3. causality; directionality (P. 105)
4. restricted range (P. 107)
5. Pearson product-moment (P. 110)
6. point-biserial (P. 112)
7. coefficient of determination (P. 112)
8. Regression analysis (P. 113)

Multiple Choice Self Test Answers

1. c (P. 101)
2. b (P. 101)
3. c (P. 101)
4. c (P. 101)
5. d (P. 103)
6. b (P. 102-103)
7. d (P. 109)
8. a (P. 108)
9. a (P. 112)
10. c (P. 112)
11. b (P. 112)
12. a (P. 113)

Key Terms

Below are the terms from the glossary presented earlier. Go through the list and see if you can remember the definition of each.

Causality
Coefficient of Determination
Correlation Coefficients
Correlational Method
Directionality
Magnitude
Negative Correlation

Partial Correlation
Pearson Product-moment
    Correlation Coefficient
Person-who Argument
Phi Coefficient
Point-biserial Correlation Coefficient
Positive Correlation

Regression Analysis
Regression Line
Restrictive Range
Scatterplot

Spearman's Rank-order Correlation
    Coefficient
Third Variable Problem

Chapter 6
Hypothesis Testing and Inferential Statistics

Chapter Outline

Chapter Summary

This chapter consisted of an introduction to hypothesis testing and inferential statistics. There was a discussion of hypothesis testing including the null and alternative hypotheses, one- and two-tailed hypothesis tests, and Type I and Type II errors in hypothesis testing. In addition, the concept of statistical significance was defined. The most simplistic use of hypothesis testing—a single-group design—in which the performance of a sample is compared to the general population was presented to illustrate the use of inferential statistics in hypothesis testing. Two parametric statistical tests were described—the z-test and the t-test. Each compares a sample mean to the general population. Because both are parametric tests, the distributions should be bell-shaped and certain parameters should be known (in the case of the z-test, μ an σ must be known; for the t-test, only μ is needed). In addition, because these are parametric tests, the data should be interval or ratio in scale. These tests involve the use of the sampling distribution (the distribution of sample means). They also involve the use of the standard error of the mean (or estimated standard error of the mean for the t-test) which is the standard deviation of the sampling distribution. Both z- and t-tests can test one- or two-tailed alternative hypotheses, but one-tailed tests are more powerful statistically.

The final inferential statistic introduced was the χ^2 goodness-of-fit test—a nonparametric test. Nonparametric tests are those for which population parameters (μ and σ) are not known. In addition, there is no assumption of normality concerning the underlying distribution of scores, and the data are most commonly nominal in nature. As such, it examines how well an observed frequency distribution of a nominal variable fits some expected pattern of frequencies.

Lastly, the concept of correlation coefficients was revisited with respect to significance testing. This involved learning how to determine whether an observed correlation coefficient is statistically significant by using a critical values table.

Learning Objectives

- Differentiate null and alternative hypotheses.

- Differentiate one- and two-tailed hypothesis tests.

- Explain how Type I and Type II errors are related to hypothesis testing.

- Explain what statistical significance means.

- Explain what a z test is and what it does.

- Calculate a z test.

- Explain what statistical power is and how to make statistical tests more powerful.

- List the assumptions of the z test.

- Explain what a t test is and what it does.

- Calculate a t test.

- List the assumptions of the t test.

- Explain what a χ^2 goodness-of-fit test is and what it does.

- Calculate a χ^2 goodness-of-fit test.

- List the assumptions of the χ^2 goodness -of-fit test.

Glossary of Important Terms

Study the list of terms below so that you could, if asked, explain them to someone else.

χ^2 **Goodness-of-Fit Test**—A nonparametric inferential procedure that determines how well an observed frequency distribution fits an expected distribution.

Alternative Hypothesis (Research Hypothesis)—The hypothesis that the researcher wants to support predicting that a significant difference exists between the groups being compared.

Critical Value—The value of a test statistic (for example a z-test) that marks the edge of the region of rejection in a sampling distribution where values equal to it or beyond it fall in the region of rejection.

Estimated Standard Error of the Mean—An estimate of the standard deviation of the sampling distribution.

Expected Frequencies—The frequency expected in a category if the sample data represent the population.

Hypothesis Testing—The process of determining whether a hypothesis is supported by the results of a research study.

Inferential Statistics—Statistics that involve the use of procedures for drawing conclusions based on the scores collected in a research study and going beyond them to make conclusions (inferences) about a population.

Nonparametric tests—Tests that do not involve the use of any population parameters—μ and σ are not needed and the underlying distribution does not have to be normal.

Null Hypothesis—The hypothesis predicting that no difference exists between the groups being compared.

Observed Frequencies—The frequency with which participants fall into a category.

One-tailed Hypothesis (Directional Hypothesis)—An alternative hypothesis in which the researcher predicts the direction of the expected difference between the groups.

Parametric tests—Tests that involve making assumptions about estimates of population characteristics or parameters.

Power—The ability to find significant differences when they truly exist.

Sampling Distribution—A distribution of sample means based on random samples of a fixed size from a population.

Single-group Design—A research study in which there is only one group of participants.

Standard Error of the Mean—The standard deviation of the sampling distribution.

Statistical Significance—An observed difference between two descriptive statistics (such as means) that is unlikely to have occurred by chance alone.

Student's *t*-distribution—A set of distributions that, although symmetrical and bell-shaped, are NOT normally distributed.

t **test**—A parametric inferential statistical test of the null hypothesis for a single sample where the population variance is not known.

Two-tailed Hypothesis (Non-directional Hypothesis)—An alternative hypothesis in which the researcher predicts that the groups being compared differ, but does not predict the direction of the difference.

Type I Error—An error in hypothesis testing in which the null hypothesis is rejected when it is true.

Type II Error—An error in hypothesis testing in which there is a failure to reject the null hypothesis when it is false.

z **test**—A parametric inferential statistical test of the null hypothesis for a single sample where the population variance is known.

Chapter Summary Matrices

Following are the summary matrices from Chapter 6. Review the material in the matrices before taking the self-tests that follow.

Hypothesis Testing

Concept	Description	Example
Null Hypothesis	The hypothesis stating that the independent variable has no effect and that there will be no difference between the two groups	$H_0: \mu_0 = \mu_1$
Alternative Hypothesis or Research Hypothesis	The hypothesis stating that the independent variable has an effect and that there will be a difference between the two groups	$H_a: \mu_0 \neq \mu_1$ (two-tailed) $H_a: \mu_0 < \mu_1$ (one-tailed) $H_a: \mu_0 > \mu_1$ (one-tailed)
Two-Tailed or Non-Directional Test	An alternative hypothesis stating that a difference is expected between the groups, but there is no prediction as to which group will perform better or worse	The mean of the sample will be different from or unequal to that of the general population
One-Tailed or Directional Test	An alternative hypothesis stating that a difference is expected between the groups, and it is expected to occur in a specific direction	The mean of the sample will be greater than the mean of the population, or the mean of the sample will be less than the mean of the population

Type I Error	The error of rejecting H_0 when we should have failed to reject it	This error in hypothesis testing is equivalent to a "false alarm", saying that there is a difference when in reality there is no difference between the groups
Type II Error	The error of failing to reject H_0 when we should have rejected it	This error in hypothesis testing is equivalent to a "miss", saying that there is not a difference between the groups when in reality there is
Statistical Significance	When the probability of a Type I error is low (less than .05)	The difference between the groups is so large that we conclude it is not due to chance

Single Sample Research and Inferential Statistics

Concept	Description	Example
Parametric Inferential Statistics	• Inferential statistical procedures that require certain assumptions about the parameters of the population represented by the sample data, such as knowing μ and σ and that the distribution is normal • Most often used with interval or ratio data	z-test t-test
Nonparametric Inferential Statistics	• Inferential procedures that do not require assumptions about the parameters of the population represented by the sample data. μ and σ are not needed and the underlying distribution does not have to be normal • Most often used with ordinal or nominal data	χ^2 Goodness-of-Fit Test

The z-test (Part I)

Concept	Description	Use
Sampling Distribution	A distribution of sample means where each sample is of the same size (n)	Used for comparative purposes for z-tests—a sample mean is compared to the sampling distribution to assess the likelihood that the sample is part of the sampling distribution

Standard Error of the Mean ($\sigma_{\overline{X}}$)	The standard deviation of a sampling distribution determined by dividing σ by $\sqrt{N}$	Used in the calculation of a z-test
z-test	Indicates the number of standard deviation units the sample mean is from the mean of the sampling distribution	An inferential test comparing a sample mean to the sampling distribution in order to determine the likelihood that the sample is part of the sampling distribution

The z-test (Part II)

Concept	Description	Example
One-Tailed z-test	A directional inferential test in which a prediction is made that the population represented by the sample will be either above or below the general population	H_a: $\mu_0 < \mu_1$ or H_a: $\mu_0 > \mu_1$
Two-Tailed z-test	A non-directional inferential test in which the prediction is made that the population represented by the sample will differ from the general population, but the direction of the difference is not predicted	H_a: $\mu_0 \neq \mu_1$
Statistical Power	The probability that the study will yield a significant result if the alternative hypothesis is true	• One-tailed tests are more powerful • Increasing sample size increases power

The t-Test

Concept	Description	Use/Example
Estimated Standard Error of the Mean ($s_{\overline{X}}$)	The estimated standard deviation of a sampling distribution. Estimated by dividing s by $\sqrt{N}$	Used in the calculation of a t-test

The *t*-test	Indicates the number of standard deviation units the sample mean is from the mean of the sampling distribution	An inferential statistical test that differs from the *z*-test in that the sample size is small (usually < 30) and σ is not known
One-Tailed *t*-test	A directional inferential test in whichh a prediction is made that the population represented by the sample will be either above or below the general population	H_a: $\mu_0 < \mu_1$ or H_a: $\mu_0 > \mu_1$
Two-Tailed *t*-test	A non-directional inferential test in which the prediction is made that the population represented by the sample will differ from the general population, but the direction of the difference is not predicted	H_a: $\mu_0 \neq \mu_1$

The χ^2 Goodness-of-Fit Test

Concept	Description
χ^2 Goodness-of-Fit Test	A nonparametric inferential hypothesis test that examines how well an observed frequency distribution of a nominal variable fits some expected pattern of frequencies
Observed Frequencies	The frequencies observed in the sample
Expected Frequencies	The frequencies expected in the sample based on some pattern of frequencies such as those in the population

Review of Formulas

z test

$$z = \frac{\overline{X} - \mu}{\sigma_{\overline{X}}} \qquad\qquad \sigma_{\overline{X}} = \frac{\sigma}{\sqrt{N}}$$

t test

$$t = \frac{\overline{X} - \mu}{s_{\overline{X}}} \qquad\qquad s_{\overline{X}} = \frac{s}{\sqrt{N}}$$

Chi-square goodness of fit test

$$\chi^2 = \sum \frac{(O - E)^2}{E}$$

Fill-in Self Test

Answer the following questions. If you have trouble answering any of the questions, re-study the relevant material before going on to the multiple choice self test.

1. The hypothesis predicting that no difference exists between the groups being compared is the _null_ .

2. An alternative hypothesis in which the researcher predicts the direction of the expected difference between the groups is a _one tailed (direct)_

3. An error in hypothesis testing in which the null hypothesis is rejected when it is true is a _Type I_ .

4. When an observed difference, say between two means, is unlikely to have occurred by chance we say that the result has _statistical sig_

5. _Nonparametric_ tests are statistical tests that do not involve the use of any population parameters.

6. A _sampling distr._ is a distribution of sample means based on random samples of a fixed size from a population.

7. The _standard error of mean_ is the standard deviation of the sampling distribution.

8. The set of distributions that, although symmetrical and bell-shaped, are not normally distributed is called the _Students t dist_

9. The _T test_ is a parametric statistical test of the null hypothesis for a single sample where the population variance is not known.

10. _Observed_ and _expected_ frequencies are used in the calculation of the χ^2 statistic.

Select the single best answer for each of the following questions. If you have trouble answering any of the questions, re-study the relevant material.

1. Inferential statistics allow us to infer something about the _____ based on the _____.
   a. sample; population
   b. population; sample
   c. sample; sample
   d. population; population

2. The hypothesis predicting that differences exist between the groups being compared is the _____ hypothesis.
   a. null
   b. alternative
   c. one-tailed
   d. two-tailed

3. Null hypothesis is to alternative hypothesis as _____ is to _____.
   a. effect; no effect
   b. Type I error; Type II error
   c. no effect; effect
   d. both b and c

4. One-tailed hypothesis is to directional hypothesis as _____ hypothesis is to _____ hypothesis.
   a. null; alternative
   b. alternative; null
   c. two-tailed; non-directional
   d. two-tailed; one-tailed

5. When using a one-tailed hypothesis the researcher predicts:
   a. the direction of the expected difference between the groups.
   b. only that the groups being compared will differ in some way.
   c. nothing.
   d. only one thing.

6. In a study on the effects of caffeine on driving performance, researchers predict that those in the group that is given more caffeine will exhibit worse driving performance. The researchers are using a _____ hypothesis.
   a. two-tailed
   b. directional
   c. one-tailed
   d. both b and c

7. A conservative statistical test is one that:
   a. minimizes both type I and type II errors.
   b. minimizes type I errors but increases type II errors.
   c. minimizes type II errors but increases type I errors.
   d. decreases the chance of type II errors.

8. In a recent study, researchers concluded that caffeine significantly increased stress levels. What the researchers were unaware of, however, was that several of the participants in the no caffeine group were also taking anti-anxiety medications. The researchers' conclusion is a _____ error.
   a. Type II
   b. Type I
   c. null hypothesis
   d. alternative hypothesis

9. When alpha is .05, this means that:
   a. the probability of a Type II error is .95.
   b. the probability of a Type II error is .05.
   c. the probability of a Type I error is .95.
   d. the probability of a Type I error is .05.

10. Parametric is to nonparametric as _____ is to _____.
   a. z test; t test
   b. t test; z test
   c. χ^2 test; z test
   d. t test; χ^2 test

11. The sampling distribution is a distribution of:
   a. sample means.
   b. population mean.
   c. sample standard deviations.
   d. population standard deviations.

12. A one-tailed z test test is to _____ whereas a two-tailed z test is to _____.
   a. $\pm 1.645; \pm1.96$
   b. $\pm1.96; \pm1.645$
   c. Type I error; Type II error
   d. Type II error; Type I error

13. Which of the following is an assumption of the t-test?
   a. The data should be ordinal or nominal.
   b. The population distribution of scores should be normal.
   c. The population mean (μ) and standard deviation (σ) are known.
   d. The sample size is typically less than 30.

14. Which of the following is an assumption of the χ^2-test?
   a. It is a parametric test.
   b. It is appropriate only for ordinal data.
   c. The frequency in each cell should be less than 5.
   d. The sample should be randomly selected.

Self Test Problems

1. A researcher is interested in whether students who play chess have higher average SAT scores than students in the general population. A random sample of 75 students who play chess is tested and has a mean SAT score of 1070. The average is 1000 ($\sigma = 200$).
   a. Is this a one or two-tailed test?
   b. What are H_0 and H_a for this study?
   c. Compute z_{obt}.
   d. What is z_{cv}?
   e. Should H_0 be rejected? What should the researcher conclude?

2. A researcher hypothesizes that people who listen to classical music have higher concentration skills than those in the general population. On a standard concentration test, the overall mean is 15.5. The researcher gave this same test to a random sample of 12 individuals who regularly listen to classical music. Their scores on the test appear below.
   16 14 20 12 25 22 23 19 17 17 21 20
   a. Is this a one or two-tailed test?
   b. What are H_0 and H_a for this study?
   c. Compute t_{obt}.
   d. What is t_{cv}?
   e. Should H_0 be rejected? What should the researcher conclude?

3. A researcher believes that the percentage of people who smoke in the South is greater than the national rate. The national rate is 15%. The researcher gathers a random sample of 110 individuals who live in the South and finds that the number who smoke is 21 out of 110.

   a. What is χ^2_{obt}?
   b. What is (are) the df for this test?
   c. What is χ^2_{cv}?
   d. What conclusion should be drawn from these results?

Answers to Self Test Questions

Fill-in Self Test Answers

1. null (P. 120)
2. one-tailed (directional) (P. 121)
3. Type I (P. 122)
4. statistical significance (P. 123)
5. Nonparametric (P. 126)
6. sampling distribution (P. 127)
7. standard error of the mean (P. 128)
8. Student's t distribution (P. 136)
9. t test (P. 136)
10. Observed; expected (P. 142)

Multiple Choice Self Test Answers

1. b (P. 120)
2. b (P. 121)
3. c (P. 121)
4. c (P. 121)
5. a (P. 121)
6. c (P. 121)
7. b (P. 122-123)
8. b (P. 122-123)
9. d (P. 123)
10. d (P. 126)
11. a (P. 127)
12. a (P. 130-132)
13. d (P. 136)
14. d (P. 144)

Answers to Self Test Problems

1. a. one-tailed
    b. H_0: $\mu_{\text{Chess}} = \mu_{\text{General Population}}$; H_a: $\mu_{\text{Chess}} > \mu_{\text{General Population}}$
    c. $z_{\text{obt}} = +3.03$
    d. $z_{\text{cv}} = \pm1.645$
    e. Reject H_0. Students who play chess score significantly higher on the SAT.
2. a. one-tailed
    b. H_0: $\mu_{\text{Classical Music}} = \mu_{\text{General Population}}$; H_a: $\mu_{\text{Classical Music}} > \mu_{\text{General Population}}$
    c. $t_{\text{obt}} = +3.05$
    d. $t_{\text{cv}} = \pm1.796$
    e. Reject H_0. Those who listen to classical music score significantly higher on the concentration test.
3. a. $\chi^2_{\text{obt}} = 1.45$
    b. df = 1
    c. $\chi^2_{\text{cv}} = 3.841$
    d. The percentage of people who smoke in the South does not differ significantly from that in the general population.

Key Terms

Below are the terms from the glossary presented earlier. Go through the list and see if you can remember the definition of each.

χ^2 Goodness-of-Fit Test
Alternative Hypothesis (Research
    Hypothesis)
Critical Value
Estimated Standard Error of the
    Mean
Expected Frequencies
Hypothesis Testing
Inferential Statistics
Nonparametric Tests
Null Hypothesis
Observed Frequencies
One-tailed Hypothesis (Directional
    Hypothesis)

Parametric Tests
Power
Sampling Distribution
Single-group Design
Standard Error of the Mean
Statistical Significance
Student's t Distribution
t-test
Two-tailed Hypothesis (Non-
    directional Hypothesis)
Type I Error
Type II Error
z-test

Chapter 7
The Logic of Experimental Design

Chapter Outline

Chapter Summary

Several factors need to be considered when designing and evaluating a true experiment. First, the issues of control and possible confounds need to be addressed. The study needs to be designed with strong control and no confounds in order to maximize internal validity. Second, external validity needs to be considered in order to ensure that the study is as generalizable as possible while maintaining control. Lastly, the design most appropriate for the type of research being conducted must be used. Researchers should consider the strengths and weaknesses of each of the three types of designs (between-, within-, and matched-participants) when determining which would be best for their study.

Learning Objectives

- Explain a between-participants design.
- Differentiate independent variable and dependent variable.
- Differentiate control group and experimental group.
- Explain random assignment.
- Explain the relationship between confounds and internal validity.
- Describe the confounds of history, maturation, testing, regression to the mean, instrumentation, mortality, and diffusion of treatment.
- Explain what experimenter effects and participant effects are and how double-blind and single-blind experiments relate to these concepts.
- Differentiate floor and ceiling effects.
- Explain external validity.
- Explain correlated-groups designs.
- Describe order effects and how counterbalancing is related to this concept.

Glossary of Important Terms

Study the list of terms below so that you could, if asked, explain them to someone else.

Between-participants Design—An experiment in which different participants are assigned to each group.

Ceiling Effect—A limitation of the measuring instrument that limits the ability of the instrument to differentiate between scores at the top of the scale.

College Sophomore Problem—The problem resulting from using mainly college sophomores as participants in research studies.

Conceptual Replication—A study based on another study that uses different methods, a different manipulation, or a different measure.

Confound—An uncontrolled extraneous variable or flaw in an experiment.

Control Group—The group of participants that serves as the baseline in a study; they do not receive any level of the independent variable.

Correlated-groups Design—Experimental designs in which the participants in the experimental and control groups are related in some way.

Counterbalancing—A mechanism for controlling order effects by either including all orders of treatment presentation or by randomly determining the order for each participant.

Dependent Variable—The variable in a study measured by the researcher.

Diffusion of Treatment—A threat to internal validity in which observed changes in the behaviors or responses of participants may be due to information received from other participants in the study.

Double-blind Experiment—An experimental procedure in which neither the experimenter nor the participant know the condition to which each participant has been assigned.

Exact Replication—Replication of a study using the same means of manipulating and measuring the variables as in the original study.

Experimental Group—The group of participants that receives some level of the independent variable.

Experimenter Effect—A threat to internal validity in which the experimenter, consciously or unconsciously, affects the results of the study.

External Validity—The extent to which the results of an experiment can be generalized.

Floor Effect—A limitation of the measuring instrument that limits the ability of the instrument to differentiate between scores at the bottom of the scale.

History Effect—A threat to internal validity where an outside event, that is not a part of the manipulation of the experiment, could be responsible for the results.

Independent Variable—The variable in a study manipulated by the researcher.

Instrumentation Effect—A threat to internal validity in which changes in the dependent variable may occur due to changes in the measuring device.

Internal Validity—The extent to which the results of an experiment can be attributed to the manipulation of the independent variable, rather than to some confounding variable.

Matched-participants Design—A type of correlated-groups design in which participants are matched between conditions on variable(s) that the researcher believes is(are) relevant to the study.

Maturation Effect—A threat to internal validity where the possibility of naturally occurring changes within the participants is responsible for the observed results.

Mortality—A threat to internal validity in which a differential drop out rate may be observed between the experimental and control groups leading to inequality between the groups.

Order Effects—A problem for within-participants designs in which the order of the conditions has an effect on the dependent variable.

Participant Effect—A threat to internal validity in which the participant, consciously or unconsciously, affects the results of the study.

Posttest-only Control Group Design—An experimental design in which the dependent variable is measured after the manipulation of the independent variable.

Pretest-posttest Control Group Design—An experimental design in which the dependent variable is measured both before and after manipulation of the independent variable.

Random Assignment—Determining who serves in each group in an experiment randomly.

Regression to the Mean—A threat to internal validity in which extreme scores, upon retesting, tend to be less extreme, moving toward the mean.

Single-blind Experiment—An experimental procedure in which the participant does not know the condition to which he has been assigned.

Systematic Replication—A study that varies from an original study in one systematic way, for example, by using a different number or type of participants, a different setting, or more levels of the independent variable.

Testing Effect—A threat to internal validity in which repeated testing leads to better or worse scores.

Within-participants Design—A type of correlated-groups design in which the same participants are used in each condition.

Chapter Summary Matrices

Following are the summary matrices from Chapter 7. Review the material in the matrices before taking the self-tests that follow.

Threats to Internal Validity

Major Confounding Variables		
Type of Confound	**Description**	**Means of Controlling/Minimizing**
Non-equivalent Control Group	Problems in participant selection or assignment may lead to important differences between the participants assigned to the experimental and control groups	Random sampling and random assignment of participants
History Effect	Changes in the dependent variable may be due to historical events that take place during the course of the study	Use of equivalent control group
Maturation Effect	Changes in the dependent variable may be due to participants maturing or growing older during the course of the study	Use of equivalent control group
Testing Effect	Changes in the dependent variable may be due to participants repeatedly being tested and hence either getting better or worse based on these repeated testings	Use of equivalent control group
Regression to the Mean	Participants who are selected for a study because they are extreme (either high or low) on some variable may regress toward the mean and be less extreme at a later testing	Use of equivalent groups of participants with extreme scores

Instrumentation Effect	Changes in the dependent variable may occur due to changes in the measuring device, either human or machine	Use of equivalent control group
Mortality or Attrition	Differential attrition or drop out between the experimental and control groups may lead to inequality between the groups	Monitoring for differential loss of participants in experimental and control groups
Diffusion of Treatment	Changes are observed in the behaviors or responses given by participants due to information they may have received from others participating in the study	Attempt to minimize by running participants all at once or as close together in time as possible
Experimenter and Participant Effects	Either experimenters or participants consciously or unconsciously affect the results of the study	Use of double-blind or single-blind procedure
Floor and Ceiling Effects	Occurs when using a measuring instrument that is not sensitive enough to detect differences	Ensuring that the measuring instrument is reliable and valid prior to beginning the study

Comparison of Designs

	Between-participants Design	Within-participants Design	Matched-participants Design
Description	Different participants are randomly assigned to each condition	The same participants are used in all conditions	Participants are randomly assigned to each condition after they are matched on relevant variables
Strengths	• Testing effects are minimized • Demand characteristics are minimized	• Fewer participants are needed • Less time consuming • Equivalency of groups is ensured • More powerful statistically	• Testing effects are minimized • Demand characteristics are minimized • Groups are fairly equivalent • More powerful statistically

Weaknesses	• **More participants are needed** • **More time consuming** • **Groups may not be equivalent** • **Less powerful statistically**	• **Probability of testing effects is high** • **Probability of demand characteristics is high**	• **Matching is very difficult** • **More participants are needed**

Fill-in Self Test

Answer the following questions. If you have trouble answering any of the questions, re-study the relevant material before going on to the multiple choice self test.

1. An experiment in which different participants are assigned to each group is a
    between part design

2. When we use *random assign*, we determine who serves in each group in an experiment randomly.

3. When the dependent variable is measured both before and after manipulation of the independent variable we are using a *pretest-post* design.

4. *Internal Val* is the extent to which the results of an experiment can be attributed to the manipulation of the independent variable, rather than to some confounding variable.

5. A(n) *maturation* is a threat to internal validity where the possibility of naturally occurring changes within the participants is responsible for the observed results.

6. If there is a problem with the measuring device then there may be a(n)
    instrumentation effect.

7. If participants talk to each other about an experiment then there may be
    diffusion of treatment

8. When neither the experimenter nor the participant know the condition to which each participant has been assigned, a *double blind* experiment is being used.

9. When the measuring device is limited in such a way that scores at the top of the scale cannot be differentiated, there is a _ceiling_ effect.

10. The extent to which the results of an experiment can be generalized is called _external validity_

11. When a study is based on another study but uses different methods, a different manipulation, or a different measure, we are conducting a _conceptual_ replication.

12. If the order of conditions affects the results in a within-participants design, then there are _order effects_

Multiple Choice Self Test

Select the single best answer for each of the following questions. If you have trouble answering any of the questions, re-study the relevant material.

1. Manipulate is to measure as _____ is to _____.
   a. independent variable; dependent variable
   b. dependent variable; independent variable
   c. control group; experimental group
   d. experimental group; control group

2. In an experimental study on the effects of stress on appetite, stress is the _____.
   a. dependent variable
   b. independent variable
   c. control group
   d. experimental group

3. In an experimental study on the effects of stress on appetite, participants are randomly assigned to either the no stress group or the stress group. These groups represent the _____ and the _____, respectively.
   a. independent variable; dependent variable
   b. dependent variable; independent variable
   c. control group; experimental group
   d. experimental group; control group

4. Within-participants design is to between participants design as _____ is to _____.
   a. using different participants in each group; using the same participants in each group
   b. using the same participants in each group; using different participants in each group
   c. matched-participants design; correlated-groups design
   d. experimental group; control group

5. The extent to which the results of an experiment can be attributed to the manipulation of the independent variable, rather than to some confounding variable refers to:
   a. external validity.
   b. generalization to populations.
   c. internal validity.
   d. both b and c.

6. Joann conducted an experiment to test the effectiveness of an antianxiety program. The experiment took place over a one-month time period. Participants in the control group and the experimental group (those who participated in the antianxiety program) recorded their anxiety levels several times each day. Joann was unaware that that midterm exams also happened to take place during the one-month time period of her experiment. Joann's experiment is now confounded by:
   a. a maturation effect.
   b. a history effect.
   c. regression to the mean.
   d. a mortality effect.

7. Joe scored very low on the SAT the first time that he took it. Based on the confound of _____, if Joe were to retake the SAT, his score should _____.
   a. instrumentation; increase
   b. instrumentation; decrease
   c. regression to the mean; increase
   d. regression to the mean; decrease

8. When the confound of mortality occurs:
   a. participants are lost equally from both the experimental and control groups.
   b. participants die as a result of participating in the experiment.
   c. participants boycott the experiment.
   d. participants are lost differentially from the experimental and control groups.

9. Controlling participant effects is to controlling experimenter effects as _____ is to _____.
    a. fatigue effects; practice effects
    b. practice effects; fatigue effects
    c. double-blind experiment; single-blind experiment
    d. single-blind experiment; double-blind experiment

10. If you were to use a bathroom scale to weigh mice in an experimental setting, your experiment would most likely suffer from a:
    a. ceiling effect.
    b. floor effect.
    c. practice effect.
    d. fatigue effect.

11. If we were to conduct a replication in which we increased the number of levels of the independent variable we would be using a(n) _____ replication.
    a. exact
    b. conceptual
    c. exact
    d. systematic

12. Most psychology experiments suffer from the _____ problem because of the type of participants used.
    a. diffusion of treatment problem
    b. college sophomore problem
    c. regression to the mean problem
    d. mortality problem

Answers to Self Test Questions

Fill-in Self Test Answers

1. between-participants design (P. 152)
2. random assignment (P. 152)
3. pretest-posttest control group design (P. 154)
4. Internal validity (P. 155)
5. maturation effect (P. 156)
6. instrumentation (P. 175)
7. diffusion of treatment (P. 157)
8. double-blind (P. 158)
9. ceiling (P. 159)

10. external validity (P. 160)
11. conceptual (P. 161)
12. order effects (P. 163)

Multiple Choice Self Test Answers

1. a (P. 152)
2. b (P. 153)
3. c (P. 152)
4. b (P. 152, 162)
5. c (P. 155)
6. b (P. 155)
7. c (P. 156)
8. d (P. 157)
9. d (P. 158)
10. b (P. 159)
11. d (P. 162)
12. b (P. 161)

Key Terms

Below are the terms from the glossary presented earlier. Go through the list and see if you can remember the definition of each.

Between-participants Design
Ceiling Effect
College Sophomore Problem
Conceptual Replication
Confound
Control Group
Correlated-groups Design
Counterbalancing
Dependent Variable
Diffusion of Treatment
Double-blind Experiment
Exact Replication
Experimental Group
Experimenter Effect
External Validity

Floor Effect
History Effect
Independent Variable
Instrumentation Effect
Internal Validity
Matched-participants Design
Maturation Effect
Mortality
Order Effects
Participant Effect
Posttest-only Control Group Design
Pretest-posttest Control Groups Design
Random Assignment
Regression to the Mean
Single-blind Experiment

Systematic Replication
Testing Effect
Within-participants Design

Chapter 8
Inferential Statistics: Two-Group Designs

Chapter Summary

Several inferential statistics used with two-group designs were presented in this chapter. The statistics varied based on the type of data collected (nominal, ordinal, interval-ratio) and whether the design was between-participants or correlated-groups. It is imperative that the appropriate statistic be used to analyze the data collected in an experiment. The first point to consider when determining which statistic to use is whether it should be a parametric or non-parametric statistic. This decision is based on the type of data collected, the type of distribution to which the data conform, and whether any parameters of the distribution are known. Second, we need to know whether the design is between-participants or correlated-groups when selecting a statistic. Using this information, it will be possible to select and conduct the statistical test most appropriate to the design and data.

Learning Objectives

- Explain when the *t* test for independent-groups should be used.
- Calculate an independent-groups *t* test.
- Interpret an independent-groups *t* test.
- Calculate and interpret Cohen's *d*.
- Explain the assumptions of the independent-groups *t* test.
- Explain when the *t* test for correlated-groups should be used.
- Calculate a correlated-groups *t* test.
- Interpret a correlated-groups *t* test.
- Explain the assumptions of the correlated-groups *t* test.
- Explain when nonparametric tests should be used.
- Calculate Wilcoxon's rank-sum test.
- Interpret Wilcoxon's rank-sum test.
- Explain the assumptions of the Wilcoxon's rank-sum test.
- Calculate the χ^2 test for independence.
- Interpret the χ^2 test for independence.
- Explain the assumptions of the χ^2 test for independence.

Glossary of Important Terms

Study the list of terms below so that you could, if asked, explain them to someone else.

Chi-square test for independence—A nonparametric inferential test used when frequency data have been collected to determine how well an observed breakdown of people over various categories fits some expected breakdown.

Cohen's *d*—An inferential statistic for measuring effect size.

Correlated-groups *t* test—A parametric inferential test used to compare the means of two related (within- or matched-participants) samples.

Difference scores—Scores representing the difference between participants' performance in one condition and their performance in a second condition.

Effect size—The proportion of variance in the dependent variable that is accounted for by the manipulation of the independent variable.

Independent-groups *t* test—A parametric inferential test for comparing sample means of two independent groups of scores.

Phi Coefficient—An inferential test used to determine effect size for a chi-square test.

Standard Error of the Difference Between Means—The standard deviation of the sampling distribution of differences between the means of independent samples in a two-sample experiment.

Standard Error of the Difference Scores—The standard deviation of the sampling distribution of mean differences between dependent samples in a two-group experiment.

Statistical Significance—An observed difference between two descriptive statistics (such as means) that is unlikely to have occurred by chance alone.

Wilcoxon's Rank-sum Test—A nonparametric inferential test for comparing sample medians of two independent groups of scores.

Chapter Summary Matrices

Following are the summary matrices from Chapter 8. Review the material in the matrices before taking the self-tests that follow.

Type of Test		
	Independent-groups *t* Test	Correlated-groups *t* Test
What It Is	A parametric test for a two group between-participants design	A parametric test for a two group within-participants or matched-participants design
What It Does	Compares performance of the two groups to determine whether they represent the same population or different populations	Analyzes whether each individual performed in a similar or different manner across conditions
Assumptions	• Interval-ratio Data • Bell-Shaped Distribution • Independent Observations • Homogeneity of Variance	• Interval-ratio Data • Bell-Shaped Distribution • Independent Observations Between Participants • Homogeneity of Variance

Nonparametric Tests

Type of Test		
	Wilcoxon rank-sum test	Chi-square test of independence
What It Is	A nonparametric test for a two-group between-participants design	A nonparametric test for a two-group between-participants design
What It Does	Will identify differences in ranks on a variable between groups	Will identify differences in frequency on a variable between groups
Assumptions	• Ordinal Data • Distribution Is Not Normal • Independent Observations	• Random Sample • Independent Observations

Review of Formulas

Independent-groups *t* test

$$t_{obt} = \frac{\overline{x}_1 - \overline{x}_2}{s_{\overline{X}_1 - \overline{X}_2}} \qquad s_{\overline{X}_1 - \overline{X}_2} = \sqrt{\frac{s_1^2}{n_1} + \frac{s_2^2}{n_2}} \qquad d = \frac{\overline{x}_1 - \overline{x}_2}{\sqrt{\frac{s_1^2}{2} + \frac{s_2^2}{2}}}$$

Correlated-groups *t* test

$$t_{obt} = \frac{\overline{d} - 0}{s_{\overline{d}}} \qquad s_{\overline{d}} = \frac{s_d}{\sqrt{n}}$$

Chi-square test for independence

$$\chi^2 = \sum \frac{(O - E)^2}{E}$$

Fill-in Self Test

Answer the following questions. If you have trouble answering any of the questions, re-study the relevant material before going on to the multiple choice self test.

1. A(n) _indep. groups t test_ is a parametric inferential test for comparing sample means of two independent groups of scores.

2. _Cohens d_ is an inferential statistic for measuring effect size with *t* tests.

3. A(n) _corr. group t test_ is a parametric inferential test used to compare the means of two related samples.

4. When using a correlated-groups *t* test we calculate _difference score_ scores representing the difference between participants' performance in one condition and their performance in a second condition.

5. The standard deviation of the sampling distribution of mean differences between dependent samples in a two-group experiment is the _standard error of diff_.

6. The nonparametric inferential statistic for comparing two-groups when ordinal data are collected is the _Wilson Rank_.

7. When frequency data are collected we use the _χ^2 for indep_ to determine how well an observed breakdown of people over various categories fits some expected breakdown.

8. Effect size for a chi-square test is determined by using the _phi coefficient_

Multiple Choice Self Test

Select the single best answer for each of the following questions. If you have trouble answering any of the questions, re-study the relevant material.

1. When comparing the sample means for two unrelated groups we use the:
   a. correlated-groups t test.
   b. independent-groups t test.
   c. Wilcoxon rank-sum test.
   d. χ^2 test for independence.

2. The value of the t test will _____ as sample variance decreases.
   a. increase
   b. decrease
   c. stay the same
   d. not be affected

3. Which of the following t test results has the greatest chance of statistical significance?
   a. $t(28) = 3.12$
   b. $t(14) = 3.12$
   c. $t(18) = 3.12$
   d. $t(10) = 3.12$

4. If the null hypothesis is false, then the t test should be:
   a. equal to 0.00.
   b. greater than 1.
   c. greater than .05.
   d. greater than .95.

5. Imagine that you conducted an independent-groups t test with 10 participants in each group. For a one-tailed test, the t_{cv} at $\alpha = .05$ would be:
   a. ±1.729.
   b. ±2.101.
   c. ±1.734.
   d. ±2.093.

6. If a researcher reported for an independent-groups t test that $t(26) = 2.90, p < .005$, how many participants were there in the study?
   a. 13
   b. 26
   c. 27
   d. 28

7. $H_a: \mu_1 \neq \mu_2$ is the _____ hypothesis for a _____-tailed test.
   a. null; two
   b. alternative; two
   c. null; one
   d. alternative; one

8. Cohen's d is a measure of _____ for a _____.
   a. significance; t test
   b. significance; χ^2 test
   c. effect size; t test
   d. effect size; χ^2 test

9. $t_{cv} = 2.15$ and $t_{obt} = -2.20$. Based on these results we _____.
   a. reject H_o
   b. fail to reject H_o
   c. accept H_o
   d. reject H_a

10. If a correlated-groups t-test and an independent-groups t test both have df=10, which experiment used fewer participants?
    a. they both used the same number of participants (n=10)
    b. they both used the same number of participants (n=11)
    c. the correlated-groups t test
    d. the independent-groups t test

11. If researchers reported that, for a correlated-groups design, $t(15) = 2.57, p<.05$, you can conclude that:
    a. a total of 16 people participated in the study.
    b. a total of 17 people participated in the study.
    c. a total of 30 people participated in the study.
    d. there is no way to determine how many people participated in the study.

12. The Wilcoxon rank-sum test is used with _____ data.
    a. interval
    b. ordinal
    c. nominal
    d. ratio

13. The calculation of the df for the _____ is (r–1)(c–1).
    a. independent-groups t test
    b. correlated-groups t test
    (c.) χ^2 test for independence
    d. Wilcoxon rank-sum test

Self Test Problems

1. A college student is interested in whether there is a difference between male and female students in the amount of time spent doing volunteer work each week. The student gathers information from a random sample of male and female students on her campus. Amount of time volunteering (in minutes) is normally distributed. The data appear below. They are measured on an interval-ratio scale and are normally distributed.

Males	Females
20	35
25	39
35	38
40	43
36	50
24	49

   a. What statistical test should be used to analyze these data?
   b. Identify H_0 and H_a for this study.
   c. Conduct the appropriate analysis.
   d. Should H_0 be rejected? What should the researcher conclude?
   e. If significant, compute the effect size and interpret this.
   f. If significant, draw a graph representing the data.

2. A researcher is interested in whether studying with music helps or hinders the learner. In order to control for differences in cognitive ability, the researcher decides to use a within-participants design. He selects a random sample of participants and has them study different material of equal difficulty in both the music and no music conditions. Participants then take a 20-item quiz on the material. The study is completely counterbalanced to control for order effects. The data appear below. They are measured on an interval-ratio scale and are normally distributed.

Music	No Music
17	17
16	18
15	17
16	17
18	19
18	18

a. What statistical test should be used to analyze these data?
b. Identify H_0 and H_a for this study.
c. Conduct the appropriate analysis.
d. Should H_0 be rejected? What should the researcher conclude?
e. If significant, draw a graph representing the data.

3. Researchers at a food company are interested in how a new ketchup made from green tomatoes (and green in color) will compare to their traditional red ketchup. They are worried that the green color will adversely affect the tastiness scores. They randomly assign participants to either the green or red ketchup condition. Participants indicate the tastiness of the sauce on a 20-point scale. Tastiness scores tend to be skewed. The scores appear below.

Green Ketchup	Red Ketchup
14	16
15	16
16	19
18	20
16	17
16	17
19	18

a. What statistical test should be used to analyze these data?
b. Identify H_0 and H_a for this study.
c. Conduct the appropriate analysis.
d. Should H_0 be rejected? What should the researcher conclude?

4. You notice at the gym that it appears that more women tend to workout together, whereas more men tend to workout alone. In order to determine whether this difference is significant, you collect data on the workout preferences for a sample of men and women at your gym. The data appear below.

	Males	Females
Together	12	24
Alone	22	10

    a.   What statistical test should be used to analyze these data?
    b.   Identify H_0 and H_a for this study.
    c.   Conduct the appropriate analysis.
    d.   Should H_0 be rejected? What should the researcher conclude?

Answers to Self Test Questions

Fill-in Self Test Answers

1. independent-groups *t* test (P. 171)
2. Cohen's *d* (P. 175)
3. correlated-groups *t* test (P. 176)
4. difference scores (P. 177)
5. standard error of the difference scores (P. 178)
6. Wilcoxon rank-sum test (P. 181)
7. χ^2 test for independence (P. 183)
8. phi coefficient (P. 183)

Multiple Choice Self Test Answers

1. b (P. 171)
2. a (P. 171)
3. a (P. 173)
4. b (P. 173)
5. c (P. 173)
6. d (P. 173)
7. b (P. 171-173)
8. c (P. 175)
9. a (P. 179-180)
10. c (P. 179-180)
11. a (P. 179180)
12. b (P. 181)
13. c (P. 182183)

Answers to Self Test Problems

1. a. An independent-groups *t* test.
    b. H_0: $\mu_1=\mu_2$, H_a: $\mu_1\neq\mu_2$
    c. $t(10) = -2.99$, $p < .02$ or $t(10) = 2.99$, $p < .02$ (depending on which mean you place first.
    d. Reject H_0. Females spend significantly more time volunteering than males.
    e. $d = 1.72$. This is a large effect size.
    f.

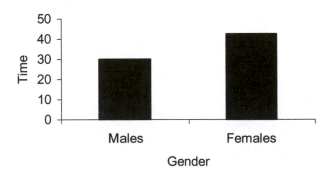

2. a. A correlated-groups *t* test.
    b. H_0: $\mu_1=\mu_2$, H_a: $\mu_1\neq\mu_2$
    c. $t(5) = 2.78$, $p < .05$.
    d. Reject H_0. When participants studied with music, they scored significantly lower on the quiz.
    e.

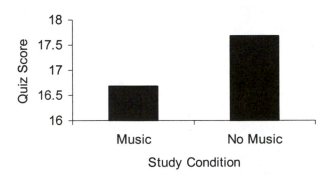

3. a. The Wilcoxon rank-sum test.
    b. H_0: $Md_{red} = Md_{green}$, H_a: $Md_{red}>Md_{green}$

c. W_s ($n_1=7$, $n_2=7$) = 41, not significant.
d. No. Fail to reject H_0. There is no significant difference in tastiness scores.

4. a. The χ^2 test for independence.
   b. H_0: There is no difference in the frequency of workout preferences for males and females.
      H_a: There is a difference in the frequency of workout preferences for males and females.
   c. χ^2 ($N=68$) = 8.5, $p < .01$.
   d. Reject H_0. There is a significant difference in the frequency of workout preferences for males and females. Females prefer to workout together more than males.

Key Terms

Below are the terms from the glossary presented earlier. Go through the list and see if you can remember the definition of each.

Chi-square Test for Independence
Cohen's *d*
Correlated-groups *t*-test
Difference Scores
Effect Size
Independent-groups *t*-test
Phi Coefficient

Standard Error of the Difference
   Between Means
Standard Error of the Difference
   Scores
Statistical Significance
Wilcoxon's Rank-sum Test

Chapter 9
Experimental Designs with More Than Two Levels of an Independent Variable

Chapter Outline

Chapter Summary

In this chapter, designs using more than two levels of an independent variable were discussed. Advantages to such designs include being able to compare more than two kinds of treatment, using fewer participants, comparing all treatments to a control group, and using placebo groups. In addition, the chapter discussed statistical analyses most appropriate for use with these designs—most commonly with interval-ratio data, an ANOVA. A randomized one-way ANOVA would be used for between-participants designs, and a repeated-measures one-way ANOVA for correlated-groups designs. Also discussed were appropriate post hoc tests (Tukey's HSD) and measures of effect size (eta-squared). Nonparametric statistics appropriate for use with ordinal (Kruskal-Wallis ANOVA) and nominal (chi-square test) data were also identified. After completing this chapter, you should appreciate the advantages of using more complicated designs and possess an understanding of the basic statistics used to analyze such designs.

Learning Objectives

- Explain what additional information can be gained by using designs with more than two levels of an independent variable.
- Identify what a one-way randomized ANOVA is and what it does.
- Use the formulas provided to calculate a one-way randomized ANOVA.
- Interpret the results from an one-way randomized ANOVA.
- Calculate Tukey's post hoc test for a one-way randomized ANOVA.
- Identify what a one-way repeated measures ANOVA is and what it does.
- Use the formulas provided to calculate a one-way repeated measures ANOVA.
- Interpret the results from an one-way repeated measures ANOVA.
- Calculate Tukey's post hoc test for a one-way repeated measures ANOVA.

Glossary of Important Terms

Study the list of terms below so that you could, if asked, explain them to someone else.

ANOVA (Analysis of Variance)—An inferential statistical test for comparing the means of three or more groups.

Between-groups Sum of Squares—The sum of squared deviations of each group's mean from the grand mean multiplied by the number of participants in each group.

Between-groups Variance—An estimate of the effect of the independent variable *and* error variance.

Bonferoni Adjustment—A means of setting a more stringent alpha level in order to minimize Type I errors.

Error Variance—The amount of variability among the scores caused by chance or uncontrolled variables.

Eta-squared—An inferential statistic for measuring effect size with an ANOVA.

F-ratio—The ratio of between-groups variance to within-groups variance.

Grand Mean—The mean performance across all participants in a study.

Mean Square—An estimate of either total variance, variance between-groups, or variance within-groups.

One-way Randomized ANOVA—An inferential statistical test for comparing the means of three or more groups using a between-participants design.

One-way Repeated Measures ANOVA— An inferential statistical test for comparing the means of three or more groups using a correlated-groups design.

Placebo—An inert substance that participants believe is a treatment.

Placebo Group— A group or condition in which participants believe they are receiving treatment but are not.

Post Hoc Tests—When using an ANOVA, a means of comparing all possible pairs of groups to determine which ones differ significantly from each other.

Total Sum of Squares—The sum of squared deviations of each score from the grand mean.

Tukey's Honestly Significant Difference—A post hoc test used with ANOVAs for making all pairwise comparisons when conditions have equal n.

Within-groups Sum of Squares—The sum of squared deviations of each score from its group mean.

Within-groups Variance—The variance within each condition; an estimate of the population error variance.

Chapter Summary Matrices

Following are the summary matrices from Chapter 9. Review the material in the matrices before taking the self-tests that follow.

Designs with more than Two Levels of an Independent Variable

Advantages	Considerations
• Allows comparisons of more than two types of treatment • Fewer participants are needed • Allows comparisons of all treatments to control condition • Allows for use of a placebo group with control and experimental groups	• Type of statistical analysis (e.g., multiple *t* tests or ANOVA) • Multiple *t* tests increase chance of Type I error; the Bonferoni adjustment increases the chance of a Type II error

Randomized One-way ANOVA

Concept	Description
Null Hypothesis (H_0)	The independent variable had no effect—the samples all represent the same population
Alternative Hypothesis (H_a)	The independent variable had an effect—at least one of the samples represents a different population than the others
F-Ratio	The ratio formed when the between-groups variance is divided by the within-groups variance
Between-groups Variance	An estimate of the variance of the group means about the grand mean. Includes both systematic variance and error variance
Within-groups Variance	An estimate of the variance within each condition in the experiment. Also known as error variance, or variance due to chance factors
Eta-squared	A measure of effect size—the variability in the dependent variable attributable to the independent variable
Tukey's Post Hoc Test	A test conducted to determine which conditions in a study with more than two groups differ significantly from each other

Repeated-measures One-way ANOVA

Concept	Description
Null Hypothesis (H_0)	The independent variable had no effect—the samples all represent the same population
Alternative Hypothesis (H_a)	The independent variable had an effect—at least one of the samples represents a different population than the others
F-Ratio	The ratio formed when the between variance is divided by the error variance
Between Variance	An estimate of the variance of the treatment means about the grand mean. Includes both systematic variance and error variance
Participant Variance	The variance due to individual differences. This is removed from the error variance
Error Variance	An estimate of the variance within each condition in the experiment after variance due to individual differences has been removed
Eta-squared	A measure of effect size—the variability in the dependent variable attributable to the independent variable
Tukey's Post Hoc Test	A test conducted to determine which conditions in a study with more than two groups differ significantly from each other

Review of Formulas

Randomized one-way ANOVA summary table, including definitional formulas.

Source	df	SS	MS	F
Between-groups	$k-1$	$\Sigma[(\overline{X}_g - \overline{X}_G)^2 \, n]$	$\dfrac{SS_b}{df_b}$	$\dfrac{MS_b}{MS_w}$
Within-groups	$N-k$	$\Sigma(X - \overline{X}_g)^2$	$\dfrac{SS_w}{df_w}$	
Total	$N-1$	$\Sigma(X - \overline{X}_G)^2$		

$$\eta^2 = \frac{SS_{Between}}{SS_{Total}} \qquad\qquad HSD_{.05} = Q(r, df_w)\sqrt{\frac{MS_w}{n}}$$

Repeated Measures one-way ANOVA summary table, including definitional formulas.

Source	df	SS	MS	F
Participant	$n-1$	$\Sigma[(\overline{X}_P - \overline{X}_G)^2\, k\,]$	$\dfrac{SS_s}{df_s}$	
Between	$k-1$	$\Sigma[(\overline{X}_t - \overline{X}_G)^2\, n\,]$	$\dfrac{SS_b}{df_b}$	$\dfrac{MS_b}{MS_e}$
Error	$(k-1)(n-1)$	$[\Sigma(X - \overline{X}_t)^2]$-$SS_P$	$\dfrac{SS_e}{df_e}$	
Total	$N-1$	$\Sigma(X - \overline{X}_G)^2$		

Fill-in Self Test

Answer the following questions. If you have trouble answering any of the questions, re-study the relevant material before going on to the multiple choice self test.

1. The _____ provides a means of setting a more stringent alpha level for multiple tests in order to minimize Type I errors.

2. A _____ is an inert substance that participants believe is a treatment.

3. A(n) _____ is an inferential statistical test for comparing the means of three or more groups.

4. The mean performance across all participants is represented by the _____.

5. The _____ variance is an estimate of the effect of the independent variable, confounds, and error variance.

6. The sum of squared deviations of each score from the grand mean is the _____.

7. When we divide an SS score by its degrees of freedom, we have calculated a _____.

8. _____ is an inferential statistic for measuring effect size with an ANOVA.

9. For an ANOVA, we use _____ to compare all possible pairs of groups to determine which ones differ significantly from each other.

10. The ANOVA for use with one independent variable and a correlated-groups design is the _____.

Multiple Choice Self Test

Select the single best answer for each of the following questions. If you have trouble answering any of the questions, re-study the relevant material.

1. The *F*-ratio is determined by dividing _____ by _____.
   a. error variance; systematic variance
   b. between-groups variance; within-groups variance
   c. within-groups variance; between-groups variance
   d. systematic variance; error variance

2. If between-groups variance is large, then we have observed:
   a. experimenter effects.
   b. large systematic variance.
   c. large error variance.
   d. possibly both b and c.

3. The larger the *F*-ratio, the greater the chance that:
   a. a mistake has been made in the computation.
   b. there are large systematic effects present.
   c. the experimental manipulation probably did not have the predicted effects.
   d. the between-groups variation is no larger than would be expected by chance alone and no larger than the within groups variance.

4. One reason to use an ANOVA over a *t* test is to reduce the risk of:
   a. a Type II error.
   b. a Type I error.
   c. confounds.
   d. error variance.

5. If the null hypothesis for an ANOVA is false, then the F-ratio should be:
   a. greater than 1.00.
   b. a negative number.
   c. 0.00.
   d. 1.00.

6. If, in a randomized ANOVA there are four groups with 15 participants in each group, then the df for the F-ratio is equal to:
   a. 60.
   b. 59.
   c. 3, 56.
   d. 3, 57.

7. For an F-ratio with df = 3, 20 the F_{cv} for α = .05 would be:
   a. 3.10.
   b. 4.94.
   c. 8.66.
   d. 5.53.

8. If a researcher reported an F-ratio with df = 2, 21 for a randomized one-way ANOVA, then there were _____ conditions in the experiment and _____ total participants.
   a. 2; 21
   b. 3; 23
   c. 2; 24
   d. 3; 24

9. Systematic variance and error variance comprise the _____ variance.
   a   within-groups
   b. total
   c. between-groups
   d. participant

10. If a randomized one-way ANOVA produced $MS_{between}$ = 25 and MS_{within} = 5, then the F-ratio would be:
    a   25/5 = 5.
    b. 5/25 = .20.
    c. 25/30 = .83.
    d. 30/5 = 6.

11. One advantage of a correlated-groups design is that the effects of _____ have been removed.
    a. individual differences
    b. experimenter effects
    c. subject bias effects
    d. measurement error

Self Test Problems

1. Calculate Tukey's HSD and eta squared for the following ANOVA.

ANOVA SUMMARY TABLE

Source	df	SS	MS	F
Participants	9	25		
Between	2	150		
Error	18	100		
Total	29			

2. The following ANOVA TABLE corresponds to an experiment on pain reliever effectiveness. Three types of pain reliever are used (aspirin, acetaminophen, and ibuprofen) and effectiveness is rated on a 0-10 scale. The scores for the six participants in each group follow:

Aspirin: 4, 6, 4, 4, 3, 5
Acetaminophen: 6, 4, 6, 7, 3, 5
Ibuprofen: 7, 6, 5, 8, 6, 5

The sums of squares are provided in the table below. However, for practice see if you can correctly calculate them by hand.

ANOVA SUMMARY TABLE

Source	df	SS	MS	F
Participants		9.12		
Between		10.19		
Error		13.90		
Total				

a. Complete the ANOVA Summary Table presented above.
b. Is F_{obt} significant at $\alpha = .05$?
c. Perform post hoc comparisons if necessary.
d. What conclusions can be drawn from the F-ratio and the post hoc comparisons?
e. What is the effect size and what does this mean?
f. Graph the means.

Answers to Self Test Questions

Fill-in Self Test Answers

1. Bonferoni adjustment (P. 193)
2. placebo (P. 195)
3. ANOVA (P. 196)
4. grand mean (P. 197)
5. between-groups (P. 198)
6. total sum of squares (P. 202)
7. mean square (P. 202)
8. Eta-squared (P. 202)
9. post hoc tests or Tukey's HSD (P. 206)
10. repeated measures ANOVA (P. 209)

Multiple Choice Self Test Answers

1. b (P. 198)
2. d (P. 198)
3. b (P. 198-199)
4. b (P. 197)
5. a (P. 198)
6. c (P. 198)
7. a (P. 198)
8. d (P. 198)
9. c (P. 197)
10. a (P. 203)
11. a (P. 208)

Answers to Self Test Problems

1. a.

Source	df	SS	MS	F
Participant	9	25		
Between	2	150		
Error	18	100		
Total	29			

$HSD_{.05} = 11.41$; $HSD_{.01} = 14.85$; eta squared = 55%.

2. a.

Source	df	SS	MS	F
Participant	5	9.12	1.82	
Between	2	10.19	5.10	3.67
Error	10	13.90	1.39	
Total	17	33.21		

Note: If calculated by hand, your SS scores may vary slightly due to rounding.

b. No, $F (2, 10) = 3.67$, not significant.
c. Post hoc tests are not necessary, but here are the answers if you want to practice--
   $HSD_{.05} = 1.86$; $HSD_{.01} = 2.53$
d. Type of pain killer did not significantly affect effectiveness rating.
e. The effect size (η^2) is 31%. Thus, knowing the type of pain killer taken can account for only 31% of the variability in effectiveness scores.
f.

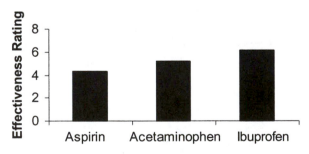

Key Terms

Below are the terms from the glossary presented earlier. Go through the list and see if you can remember the definition of each.

ANOVA (Analysis of Variance)
Between-groups Sum of
Squares
Between-groups Variance
Bonferoni Adjustment
Error Variance
Eta-squared
F-ratio
Grand Mean
Mean Square
One-way Randomized ANOVA

One-way Repeated Measures
ANOVA
Placebo
Placebo Group
Post Hoc Tests
Total Sum of Squares
Tukey's Honestly Significant
Difference
Within-groups Sum of Squares
Within-groups Variance

Chapter 10
Complex Experimental Design

Chapter Summary

In this chapter, designs using more than one independent variable were described. The chapter discussed several advantages of using such designs and introduced the concepts of factorial notation, main effects, and interaction effects. After reading the section on main and interaction effects, you should be able to graph data from a factorial design and interpret what the graph means. Additional topic coverage included the statistical analysis of such designs using a two-way ANOVA. The various calculations necessary to compute a two-way randomized ANOVA were presented along with the assumptions of the test and a description of how to interpret the results.

Learning Objectives

- Explain factorial notation and the advantages of factorial designs.

- Identify main effects and interaction effects based on looking at graphs.
- Draw graphs for factorial designs based on matrices of means.
- Explain what a two-way randomized ANOVA is and what it does.
- Calculate a two-way randomized ANOVA.
- Interpret a two-way randomized ANOVA.
- Explain what a two-way repeated measures ANOVA is.

Glossary of Important Terms

Study the list of terms below so that you could, if asked, explain them to someone else.

Factorial Design—A design with more than one independent variable.

Factorial Notation—The notation that indicates how many independent variables were used in a study and how many levels were used for each variable.

Interaction Effect—The effect of each independent variable across the levels of the other independent variable.

Main Effect—An effect of a single independent variable.

Sum of Squares Error—The sum of the squared deviations of each score from its group (cell) mean.

Sum of Squares Factor A—The sum of the squared deviation scores of each group mean for Factor A minus the grand mean times the number of scores in each Factor A condition.

Sum of Squares Factor B—The sum of the squared deviation scores of each group mean for Factor B minus the grand mean times the number of scores in each Factor B condition.

Sum of Squares Interaction—The sum of the squared difference of each condition mean minus the grand mean times the number of scores in each condition. The SS_A and SS_B are then subtracted from this.

Chapter Summary Matrices

Following are the summary matrices from Chapter 10. Review the material in the matrices before taking the self-tests that follow.

Complex Designs

	Description	Advantage or Example
Factorial Design	Any design with more than one independent variable	In the example in this chapter, word type and rehearsal type were both manipulated in order to assess main effects and whether there is an interaction effect. The advantage of this is that it more closely resembles the real world because the results are due to more than one factor (variable)
Factorial Notation	The numerical notation corresponding to a factorial design—it indicates, in brief form, the number of independent variables, and the number of levels of each variable	In a 3 x 4 design, there are two independent variables, one with three levels and one with four levels
Main Effect	An effect of a single independent variable—a main effect describes the effect of a single variable, as if there were no other variables in the study	In a study with two independent variables, there is the possibility for two main effects, one for each variable
Interaction Effect	The effect of each independent variable at the levels of the other independent variable	Interaction effects allow us to assess whether the effect of one variable depends on the level of the other variable—in this way, they allow us to more closely simulate the real world where multiple variables may interact.

Two-way Randomized ANOVA

Concept	Description
Null Hypothesis (H_0)	The independent variable had no effect—the samples all represent the same population—in a two-way ANOVA there are three null hypotheses: one for Factor A, one for Factor B, and one for the interaction of A and B
Alternative Hypothesis (H_a)	The independent variable had an effect—at least one of the samples represents a different population than the others—in a two-way ANOVA there are three alternative hypotheses: one for Factor A, one for Factor B, and one for the interaction of A and B
F-Ratio	The ratio formed when the between-groups variance is divided by the within-groups variance—in a two-way ANOVA there are three F-ratios: one for Factor A, one for Factor B, and one for the interaction of A and B

Between-groups Variance	An estimate of the variance of the group means about the grand mean—in a two-way ANOVA there are three type of between-groups variance: that attributable to Factor A, that attributable to Factor B, and that attributable to the interaction of A and B
Within-groups Variance	An estimate of the variance within each condition in the experiment—also known as error variance, or variance due to chance factors
Eta-squared	A measure of effect size—the variability in the dependent variable attributable to the independent variable—in a two-way ANOVA eta-squared is calculated for Factor A, for Factor B, and for the interaction of A and B
Tukey's Post Hoc Test	A test conducted to determine which conditions from a variable with more than two conditions differ significantly from each other

Review of Formulas

Two-way randomized ANOVA summary table, including definitional formulas.

Source	df	SS	MS	F
Factor A (Word Type)	$A-1$	$\Sigma[(\overline{X}_A - \overline{X}_G)^2\, n_A]$	$\dfrac{SS_A}{df_A}$	$\dfrac{MS_A}{MS_{Error}}$
Factor B (Rehearsal Type)	$B-1$	$\Sigma[(\overline{X}_B - \overline{X}_G)^2\, n_B]$	$\dfrac{SS_B}{df_B}$	$\dfrac{MS_B}{MS_{Error}}$
A x B	$(A-1)(B-1)$	$[\Sigma(\overline{X}_C - \overline{X}_G)^2\, n_C] - SS_A - SS_B$	$\dfrac{SS_{AxB}}{df_{AxB}}$	$\dfrac{MS_{AxB}}{MS_{Error}}$
Error	$AB(n-1)$	$\Sigma(X - \overline{X}_C)^2$	$\dfrac{SS_{Error}}{df_{Error}}$	
Total	$N-1$	$\Sigma(X - \overline{X}_G)^2$		

Fill-in Self Test

Answer the following questions. If you have trouble answering any of the questions, re-study the relevant material before going on to the multiple choice self test.

1. The notation that indicates how many independent variables were used in a study and how many levels there were for each variable is called _____.

2. An effect of a single independent variable is a _____.

3. In a 4 × 6 there are _____ independent variables, one with _____ levels and one with _____ levels.

4. In a two-way randomized ANOVA there is the possibility for _____ main effect(s) and _____ interaction effects.

5. In a two-way ANOVA, the sum of the squared deviations of each score minus its cell mean is the _____.

6. In an ANOVA we use _____ to measure effect size.

Multiple Choice Self Test

Select the single best answer for each of the following questions. If you have trouble answering any of the questions, re-study the relevant material.

1. When we manipulate more than one independent variable in a study, we:
   a. will have significant main effects.
   b. will have at least one significant interaction effect.
   c. are using a factorial design.
   d. all of the above.

2. In a study examining the effects of time of day (morning, afternoon, or evening) and teaching style (lecture only versus lecture with small group discussion) on student attentiveness, how many main effects are possible?
   a. 3
   b. 6
   c. 5
   d. 2

3. In a study examining the effects of time of day (morning, afternoon, or evening) and teaching style (lecture only versus lecture with small group discussion) on student attentiveness, how many interaction effects are possible?
   a. 1
   b. 2
   c. 6
   d. 5

4. In a study examining the effects of time of day (morning, afternoon, or evening) and teaching style (lecture only versus lecture with small group discussion) on student attentiveness, the factorial notation would be:
   a. 2×2.
   b. 2×3.
   c. 2×5.
   d. 3×3.

5. A $2 \times 4 \times 5 \times 6$ factorial design has _____ potential main effects.
   a. 2
   b. 3
   c. 4
   d. 24

6. An experiment with three independent variables each with three levels is a _____ design.
   a. 2×3
   b. 3×3
   c. $2 \times 2 \times 2$
   d. $3 \times 3 \times 3$

7. If the lines in a graph are not parallel, then there is most likely a(n):
   a. main effect of variable A.
   b. main effect of variable B.
   c. interaction effect.
   d. all of the above.

8. A two-way randomized ANOVA is to _____ as a two-way repeated measures ANOVA is to _____.
   a. two independent variables manipulated between-participants; two dependent variables manipulated within-participants
   b. two dependent variables manipulated between-participants; two independent variables manipulated within-participants
   c. two independent variables manipulated between-participants; two independent variables manipulated within-participants
   d. two dependent variables manipulated between-participants; two dependent variables manipulated within-participants

9. When the effect of one independent variable depends on the level of the other independent variable we have observed a(n):
   a. main effect of one variable.
   b. main effect of a level of an independent variable.
   c. interaction effect.
   d. all of the above.

10. How many conditions would there be in a factorial design with three levels of factor A and three levels of factor B?
    a. 6
    b. 3
    c. 9
    d. unable to determine

11. In a study with two levels of factor A, four levels of factor B, and 5 participants in each condition, the df error would be:
    a. 39.
    b. 32.
    c. 8.
    d. 40.

12. In a study with two levels of factor A, four levels of factor B, and 5 participants in each condition, the dfs for factors A and B respectively would be _____ and _____.
    a. 2; 4
    b. 4; 4
    c. 1; 4
    d. 1; 3

Self Test Problems

1. The following ANOVA Table corresponds to an experiment with two factors; 1) Time of Day (morning, afternoon, or evening) and 2) Type of Teaching Method (lecture only or lecture with small group activities). The attention level (on a 0-10 scale) of college students during the morning, afternoon, or evening is measured in each of the teaching method conditions. This is a completely between-participants design. The scores for the five participants in each group follow:

   Lecture Only/Morning: 8, 9, 9, 9, 10
   Lecture Only/Afternoon: 5, 6, 7, 8, 9
   Lecture Only/Evening: 5, 5, 6, 7, 7
   Lecture-Small Group/Morning: 3, 4, 5, 6, 7
   Lecture-Small Group/Afternoon: 5, 6, 6, 6, 7
   Lecture-Small Group/Evening: 7, 7, 8, 9, 9

   The sums of squares are provided in the table below. However, for practice see if you can correctly calculate them by hand.

ANOVA SUMMARY TABLE

Source	df	SS	MS	F
A (Time)		1.67		
B (Teaching Method)		7.50		
A x B		45.02		
Within		32.00		
Total				

   a. Construct the matrix showing the means in each cell and provide the factorial notation.
   b. Complete the ANOVA Summary Table presented above.
   c. Are the F_{obt} significant at $\alpha = .05$?
   d. What conclusions can be drawn from the F-ratio?
   e. What is the effect size and what does this mean?
   f. Graph the means.

Answers to Self Test Questions

Fill-in Self Test Answers

1. factorial notation (P. 222)
2. main effect (P. 223)
3. 2; 4; 6 (P. 223)
4. 2; 1 (P. 229)
5. SS_{Error} (P. 233)
6. eta-squared (P. 237)

Multiple Choice Self Test Answers

1. c (P. 222)
2. d (P. 223)
3. a (P. 223)
4. b (P. 223)
5. c (P. 23)
6. b (P. 225)
7. c (P. 229, 238)
8. c (P. 223)
9. c (P. 223)
10. c (P. 223)
11. b (P. 231-234)
12. d (P. 231-234)

Answers to Self Test Problems

1. a.

	Morning	Afternoon	Evening
Lecture only	9	7	6
Lecture/small-group	5	6	8

This is a 2 × 3 factorial design.

b.

ANOVA SUMMARY TABLE

Source	df	SS	MS	F
A (Time)	2	1.67	.835	.63
B (Teaching Method)	1	7.50	7.50	5.64
A x B	2	45.02	22.51	16.92
Within	24	32.00	1.33	
Total	29	86.19		

Note: If calculated by hand, your SS scores may vary slightly due to rounding.

c. Factor A: F (2, 24) = .63, not significant.
Factor B: F (1, 24) = 5.64, $p < .05$.
Interaction: F (2, 24) = 16.92, $p < .01$.

d. There is no significant effect of time of day on attentiveness. There is a significant effect of teaching method on attentiveness such that those in the lecture only groups were more attentive. There is a significant interaction effect such that as the time of day increased, attentiveness decreased for the lecture only conditions whereas as time of day increased, attentiveness increased for the lecture with small-group activities conditions.

e. The effect size (η^2) is 2% for time of day (time of day accounts for less than 2% of the variability in attentiveness scores), 9% for teaching method (teaching method accounts for 9% of the variability in attentiveness scores), and 52% for the interaction (the interaction of time of day and teaching method accounts for 52 % of the variability in attentiveness scores).

f.

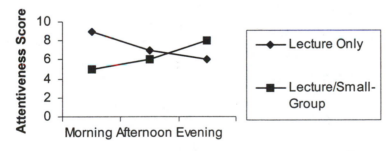

117

Key Terms

Below are the terms from the glossary presented earlier. Go through the list and see if you can remember the definition of each.

Factorial Design
Factorial Notation
Interaction Effect
Main Effect
Sum of Squares Error

Sum of Squares Factor A
Sum of Squares Factor B
Sum of Squares Interaction

Chapter 11
Quasi-Experimental and Single-Case Designs

Chapter Summary

In this chapter, you have been introduced to quasi-experimental designs—a type of design that falls somewhere between a correlational design and a true experimental design—and single-case designs. Important concepts related to quasi-experimental designs discussed include nonmanipulated independent variables (participant variables), internal validity, and confounds. Quasi-experimental designs include both single-group designs and non-equivalent control group designs. Single-case or small-*n* designs include reversal designs and multiple-baseline designs. In a reversal design, the independent variable is introduced and then removed (possibly several times) in order to assess its effect on the single participant in the study. In a multiple-baseline design, the independent variable is introduced at different times across a few participants, behaviors, or situations.

Learning Objectives

- Describe how quasi-experimental designs differ from correlational and experimental designs.
- Explain what a participant variable is.
- Differentiate single group designs and nonequivalent control group designs.
- Describe advantages and disadvantages of posttest only designs and pretest/posttest designs.
- Explain a time series design.
- Describe advantages and disadvantages of ABA versus ABAB reversal designs.
- Differentiate multiple-baseline designs (i.e., across participants, across behaviors, and across situations).

Glossary of Important Terms

Study the list of terms below so that you could, if asked, explain them to someone else.

ABA Reversal Design—A single-case design in which baseline measures are taken, the independent variable is introduced and behavior is measured, and the independent variable is then removed and baseline measures taken again.

ABAB Reversal Design—A design in which baseline and independent variable conditions are reversed twice.

Multiple-baseline Design Across Behaviors—A single-case design in which measures are taken at baseline and after the introduction of the independent variable at different times across multiple behaviors.

Multiple-baseline Design Across Participants—A small-n design in which measures are taken at baseline and after the introduction of the independent variable at different times across multiple participants.

Multiple-baseline Design Across Situations—A single-case design in which measures are taken at baseline and after the introduction of the independent variable at different times across multiple situations.

Multiple-baseline Design—A single-case or small-*n* design in which the introduction of the independent variable is assessed over multiple participants, behaviors, or situations.

Multiple-group Time-series Design—A design in which measures are taken on two or more groups both before and after a treatment.

Non-equivalent Control Group Posttest Only Design—A design in which at least two non-equivalent groups are given a treatment and then a posttest measure.

Non-equivalent Control Group Pretest-posttest Design—A design in which at least two non-equivalent groups are given a pretest, then a treatment, and then a posttest measure.

Non-manipulated Independent Variable—A design in which participants are assigned to groups based on a preexisting variable rather than being randomly assigned to the groups.

Reversal Design—A single-case design in which the independent variable is introduced and removed one or more times.

Single-case Design—A design in which only one participant is used.

Single-group Posttest Only Design—A design in which a single group of participants is given a treatment and then tested.

Single-group Pretest-posttest Design—A design in which a single group of participants takes a pretest, then receives some treatment, and then takes a posttest measure.

Single-group Time-series Design—A design in which a single group of participants is measured repeatedly before and after a treatment.

Small-*n* Design—A design in which a few participants are studied.

Chapter Summary Matrices

Following are the summary matrices from Chapter 11. Review the material in the matrices before taking the self-tests that follow.

Quasi-experimental versus Correlational Methods

	Variables	Conclusions	Cautions
Correlational Method	Two measured dependent variables	That variables may be related in some way	Cannot conclude that the relationship is causal
Quasi-experimental Method	• Typically one non-manipulated independent variable • One measured dependent variable	That systematic differences have been observed between two or more groups but cannot say that non-manipulated independent variable definitely caused the differences	Due to the confounds inherent with the use of non-manipulated independent variables, there are alternative explanations for the results

Types of Quasi-Experimental Designs

Differences in Time of Test	Group Differences	
	Single-Group	Non-Equivalent Control Group
Posttest Only	• Open to many confounds • No comparison group • No equivalent control group	• Control group is non-equivalent • No pretest measures to establish equivalence of groups • Can compare groups on posttest measures, however, differences could be due to confounds or to treatment
Pretest-Posttest	• Compare scores on pretest to those on posttest • No equivalent control group for comparison • If change is observed— may be due to treatment or confounds	• Can compare between groups on pretest and posttest • Can compare within groups from pretest to posttest • Because participants are not randomly assigned to groups, cannot say that they are equivalent • If change is observed—may be due to treatment or confounds

Time-Series	• Many measures taken, hence, can see effect of treatment over time • No control group for comparison • If change is observed—may be due to treatment or confounds	• Many measures taken, hence, can see effect of treatment over time • Non-equivalent control group available for comparison • Because participants are not randomly assigned to groups, cannot say that they are equivalent • If change is observed—may be due to treatment or confounds

Single-case Designs

Types of Single-case Designs	
Reversal Designs	**Multiple-baseline Designs**
ABA Design—measures taken at baseline, after introduction of independent variable, and at baseline again	Across Participants—measures taken at baseline and after introduction of independent variable at different times across multiple participants
ABAB Design—measures taken at baseline, after introduction of independent variable, at baseline again ,and after introduction of independent variable again	Across Behaviors—measures taken at baseline and after introduction of independent variable at different times across multiple behaviors
	Across Situations—measures taken at baseline and after introduction of independent variable at different times across multiple situations

Fill-in Self Test

Answer the following questions. If you have trouble answering any of the questions, re-study the relevant material before going on to the multiple choice self test.

1. A _____ variable is a characteristic inherent in the participants that cannot be changed.

2. The _____ design involves giving a treatment to a single group of participants and then testing them.

3. A design in which a single group of participants is measured repeatedly before and after a treatment is a _____ design.

4. A design in which at least two nonequivalent groups are given a pretest, then a treatment, and then a posttest measure is a _____ design.

5. A design in which only one participant is used is called a _____ design.

6. A design in which a few participants are studied is called a _____ design.

7. A single-case design in which baseline measures are taken, the independent variable is introduced and behavior is measured, and the independent variable is then removed and baseline measures taken again is a(n) _____ design.

8. A small-*n* design in which measures are taken at baseline and after the introduction of the independent variable at different times across multiple participants is a _____ design.

Multiple Choice Self Test

Select the single best answer for each of the following questions. If you have trouble answering any of the questions, re-study the relevant material.

1. When using a _____ variable, participants are _____ assigned to groups.
    a. nonmanipulated independent; randomly
    b. nonmanipulated independent; not randomly
    c. participant; not randomly
    d. both b and c

2. Which of the following is a participant variable?
    a. ethnicity
    b. gender
    c. age
    d. all of the above

3. Correlational research differs from quasi-experimental research in that:
   a. with correlational research we measure two variables.
   b. with quasi-experimental research there is one nonmanipulated independent variable and one measured variable.
   c. with quasi-experimental research there is one manipulated independent variable and one measured variable.
   d. both a and b.

4. Students in one of Mr. Kirk's classes participate in new interactive history learning modules. Students in another class learn history using the traditional lecture method. After three months, all students take a test to assess their knowledge of history. What kind of design did Mr. Kirk use?
   a. nonequivalent control group posttest only design
   b. nonequivalent control group pretest-posttest design
   c. multiple-group time-series design
   d. single-group time-series design

5. A problem with nonequivalent control group designs is that:
   a. they are open to many confounds.
   b. there is no comparison group.
   c. there is no equivalent control group.
   d. both a and c.

6. The difference between pretest/posttest designs and time-series design is that time series design take _____ measures.
   a. fewer
   b. more
   c. the same number of
   d. more reliable

7. Which of the following is a type of single-case design?
   a. ABA reversal designs
   b. multiple baseline across participants
   c. time-series design
   d. single-group posttest only design

8. The ABA design is generally considered _____ than the ABAB design because participants _____.
   a. more desirable; are left with the effects of the treatment
   b. less desirable; are not left with the effects of the treatment
   c. more desirable; are not left with the effects of the treatment
   d. less desirable; are left with the effects of the treatment

Answers to Self Test Questions

Fill-in Self Test Answers

1. participant (P. 244)
2. single-group posttest only (P. 247)
3. time-series (P. 248)
4. nonequivalent control group pretest/posttest (P. 249)
5. single-case (P. 253)
6. small-*n* (P. 253)
7. ABA reversal (P. 254)
8. multiple baseline across participants (P. 256)

Multiple Choice Self Test Answers

1. d (P. 244)
2. d (P. 244)
3. d (P. 244)
4. a (P. 249)
5. d (P. 249)
6. b (P. 248-249)
7. a (P. 253)
8. b (P. 254)

Key Terms

Below are the terms from the glossary presented earlier. Go through the list and see if you can remember the definition of each.

ABA Reversal Design
ABAB Reversal Design
Multiple-baseline Design
Multiple-baseline Design Across Behaviors
Multiple-baseline Design Across
   Participants
Multiple-baseline Design Across Situations
Multiple-group Time-series Design
Nonequivalent Control Group
   Posttest Only Design

Nonequivalent Control Group
   Pretest-posttest Design
Non-manipulated Independent Variable
Reversal Design
Single-case Design
Single-group Posttest Only Design
Single-group Pretest-posttest Design
Single-group Time-series Design
Small-*n* Design

Chapter 12
APA Guidelines: Ethics and Writing

Chapter Summary

After reading this chapter, you should have an understanding of APA's ethical principles and writing standards. In reviewing ethical guidelines for using humans for research purposes, the importance of IRBs and obtaining informed consent, which is a necessity when participants are at risk, were discussed. Also considered was the use of deception in research, along with the nature and intent of debriefing participants. Finally, special considerations when using children as research participants and the APA guidelines on the use of animals in research were presented.

In the second half of the chapter, basic APA formatting and writing guidelines were presented. This included how to write clearly, avoid grammatical problems, report numbers, and properly cite and reference the works of others. Finally, the organization of an APA style manuscript was described, with frequent references to the sample paper in Appendix D.

Learning Objectives

- Briefly describe APA ethical standards in research with human participants.
- Explain what an IRB is.
- Explain when deception is acceptable in research.
- Identify what it means to be a participant at risk versus a participant at minimal risk.
- Explain why debriefing is important.
- Briefly describe the ethical standards in research with animals.
- Identify and briefly describe the basic components of a APA format paper.

Glossary of Important Terms

Study the list of terms below so that you could, if asked, explain them to someone else.

Debriefing—Providing information about the true purpose of the study as soon after the completion of data collection as possible.

Deception—Lying to the participants concerning the true nature of the study because knowing the true nature of the study would affect how they might perform in the study.

Informed Consent—A form given to individuals before they participate in a study in order to inform them of the general nature of the study and to obtain their consent to participate.

Institutional Review Board—A committee charged with evaluating research projects in which human participants are used.

Fill-in Self Test

Answer the following questions. If you have trouble answering any of the questions, re-study the relevant material before going on to the multiple choice self test.

1. The form given to individuals before they participate in a study in order to inform them of the general nature of the study and to obtain their consent to participate is called a(n)

   _____.

2. Lying to the participants concerning the true nature of the study because knowing the true nature of the study would affect how they might perform in the study involves using

   _____.

3. A(n) _____ is the committee charged with evaluating research projects in which human participants are used.

4. The subsections in a methods section of an APA format paper include the

   _____.

5. Statistical findings are reported in the _____ section of an APA format paper.

6. The page after the title page in an APA format paper is always the _____.

Multiple Choice Self Test

Select the single best answer for each of the following questions. If you have trouble answering any of the questions, re-study the relevant material.

1. The Milgram obedience to authority study is to _____ as the Tuskegee syphilis study is to _____.
   a. the use of deception; participant selection problems
   b. failure to use debriefing; the use of deception
   c. the use of deception; failure to obtain informed consent
   d. failure to obtain informed consent; the use of deception

2. Debriefing involves:
   a. explaining the purpose of a study to subjects after completion of data collection.
   b. having the participants read and sign an informed consent before the study begins.
   c. lying to the participants about the true nature of the study.
   d. none of the above.

3. An institutional review board reviews research proposals to ensure:
   a. that ethical standards are met.
   b. that the proposal is methodologically sound.
   c. that enough participants are being used.
   d. that there will be no legal ramifications from the study.

4. _____ is to research involving no more risk than that encountered in daily life as _____ is to being placed under some emotional or physical risk.
   a. Moderate risk; minimal risk
   b. Risk; minimal risk
   c. Minimal risk; risk
   d. Minimal risk; moderate risk

5. A description of prior findings in the area of study is to the _____ as a report of statistical findings is to _____.
   a. introduction; method section
   b. method section; introduction
   c. introduction; results section
   d. results section; method section

6. A summary of the entire research project is to _____ as an interpretation of the findings is to _____.
   a. abstract; results section
   b. method section; results section
   c. abstract; discussion section
   d. results; discussion section

7. Which list below represents the correct ordering of the sections of an APA paper?
    a. abstract, method, introduction, results
    b. introduction, abstract, method, results
    c. discussion, abstract, introduction, method
    d. title page, abstract, introduction, method

8. Based on APA style, what is wrong with the following reference?

   Karau, Steven. J., & Williams, Kenneth. D. (1993). Social loafing: A meta-analytic

   review and theoretical integration. *Journal of Personality and Social Psychology, 65,*

   681-706.

    a. The name of the journal should be underlined.
    b. Only the initials for the authors' first and middle names should be used.
    c. The first letters of the words in the title of the paper should be capitalized.
    d. Nothing is wrong with the reference.

Answers to Self Test Questions

Fill-in Self Test Answers

1. informed consent (P. 267)
2. deception (P. 269)
3. institutional review board (IRB) (P. 267)
4. participants, apparatus/materials, procedure (P. 282)
5. results (P. 282)
6. abstract (P. 284)

Multiple Choice Self Test Answers

1. c (P. 262-263)
2. a (P. 269)
3. a (P. 267)
4. c (P. 268-269)
5. c (P. 282)
6. c (P. 281, 283)
7. d (P. 281, 283)

8.   b (P. 279)

Key Terms

Below are the terms from the glossary presented earlier. Go through the list and see if you can remember the definition of each.

Debriefing
Deception
Informed Consent
Institutional Review Board (IRB)